WIDENING UNDERGROUND (Vol 4)

(Third edition) Copyright AG Enterprises 2017

Extracts from the World-famous website:

CONTENTS

Home

Welcome to one of the most unusual and intriguing sites on the net.

The **Literature** section comprises a number of different HIVES each containing a selection of short stories, poems, and political satire.

There is also a section involving **Prophecy and Prediction**, *Spells and Invocations*.

You can also order your own personalised <u>ASBO.</u>

I have long considered writing to be a form of art.

The Artwork section contains pages from the infamous 'THUNDERBUCK RAM.'

BELINDA'S HOT AIR gives participants of the site the opportunity to express their views on a very diverse range of subjects.   By clicking on the heading you can add your own comments, but you need to be signed in to Facebook.
FIRST CONTACT is a forum for new untested art forms and experimental writing.

In an age of increasing state control and monitoring your general comments and feedback are positively encouraged.
Our freedom of speech and liberal values have to be permanently fought for or else they are lost.

live dangerously and to your heart be true.

Proxima Centauri Alpha L0+4A

INTRO

'Airing the 'Arris' (the original title for this collection)

Many years ago I went to look after a lady suffering from MS the other side of London. I stopped all Christmas with her family. They treated me like one of their own. At three o'clock every afternoon we hoisted her up from the wheelchair and pulled down her knickers. As she dangled in mid-air she shouted: "Time to air the 'Arris," but I think 'Arris' should have been spelt with a 'H.'

GENERAL MAYHEM

'Each night the Sun dies and travels through the Underworld, only to be reborn each dawn. Perhaps, like the Phoenix, I will rise again.' Landru

WWW.LANDRUCUCHULAINSTARWORD.CO.UK

With regard to (2) exhibits by Mrs Harrison (date 6 October 2015)

I am unaware of any noise nuisance on these dates.

Signed: **Bunderchook**

Date: 2nd February 2016

Dear Court,

Regarding Wherry/Circle Housing _versus_ the Beast

Before **Judge McLoughlin:**

I wish to appeal against this unjust and wholly inexcusable decision on the following grounds:

1 It _was_ unjust and unfair: Judge McLoughlin did not seem to want to hear our side of the story, was impatient and lacking in understanding.

*Judge McLoughlin was prejudiced against me from the start due to certain disclosures made by me to the Court prior to the hearing. Circle Housing were also quick to tell the tale.

2 Judge McLoughlin based his decision on the fact that I broken the law in the past, which had nothing at all to do with the complaint of so-called 'noise disturbance,' in which case I could not possibly have had a fair hearing.

3 While representing myself I was left out of any discussions between the Judge and the Complainant's Representative either before, during or after the hearing.

4 I was not allowed to finish cross-examining one of the Witness's who had been telling lies about me and who had been very insulting in the Courtroom. What has having a "hairy back" got to do with anything? The Witness continued to barrack me throughout and repeatedly fired back questions of his own. It was obvious to anyone there that the Witness had some kind of grudge against me, but this was totally disregarded. The Judge also ignored his obvious collusion with the main Complainant.

5 I was not allowed to question some of the other _Witnesses_ sneering at the back of the Court-room.

6 My chief witness was discredited due to her naivety and lack of understanding. She was labelled a liar by the Judge, as were my mother, Mrs Lodge (who could not be there) and myself, even though the Judge knew full well we were telling the truth.

*It appeared from the Judge's comments that he completely went along with the Housing Association's claim that I had encouraged my Partner to tell lies. The Judge made no comment about either her forthright denial that I had not banged on the wall in the middle of the night, or my forthright denial that I had been at home in bed on each and every occasion. The Judge sided with the Complainants even though we knew for a fact they were lying.

7 My own words: "sometimes I don't always see myself as others see me," which I had written in private to the Judge were quoted by him against me.

8 I was not able to call on other Witnesses to give evidence in person.

9 It is totally against my human rights and the rights of my partner to stop me seeing her at her bungalow when I have done nothing wrong.

10 The Judge only seemed to want to listen to the lies coming from the Housing Association. He took no notice of my assertion that the Support Manager (Mrs Bryant) had lied in Court. Records will show that she actually changed her story from the one she had previously invented. Much was made of her claim that I had thrown some keys on the table nine months ago and said in anger: "Your time will come!"

11 There was no actual proof that what the Claimant's said was true. The decision was based on lies, perjury and deceit. Not that this would ever worry a Judge in his lavish mansion, or in his Rolls Royce, on the way to the local brothel.

12 Judge McLoughlin had no intention of doing anything other than granting the order because of what had previously been said about me behind closed doors.

13 Judge McLoughlin took no notice of the fact that we had been willing to go to an outside Mediator arranged by Wherry Housing long before it got to the stage of going to Court.

14 The Judge took no notice of slanderous remarks being put around by some of the Claimants i.e. that I had been evicted, or that I had damaged cars in the car park and been stalking some of the nearby Residents (all of which were utterly untrue).

15 There was not a single scrap of evidence that I was there when the complaints of noise were made. I was in fact at home.

16 The Judge did not take any notice of my references or the fact that I had done a lot of charitable work to help the Residents while I was living at *Bure Valley Shithouse*.

He was only interested in my 'label.' I admitted long ago that I had been sent to prison for contacting my ex partner on the phone (over seven years ago) and that I had been suffering from continual harassment from the police ever since. The same police who had been going around spreading stories about me to all my ex neighbours with the encouragement of Wherry Housing.

The thousand mile exclusion zone which Wherry asked for seems typically harsh of an organisation famed for its 'specialist care…'

What would happen if my partner became seriously ill at home?

I would not be able to see her. This just shows what a load of bullshit this all is.

Whereas I do not expect the decision to be reversed by any appeal to other cronies in the Establishment it would be wrong not to appeal against the lies which have been told about me.

NB I would rather Mrs Didwell's phone number had not be included in the exhibits because she is just likely to accuse me of malicious phone calls next.

Trump gunned down by Koran wielding meer-kat

It's only a matter of time I feel, before Donald Trump meets the same fate as JFK. I can't imagine any Politician surviving for too long who speaks the truth and is also a Fascist. It would be interesting to see him speak in Blackburn, or Bradford or Birmingham. Surely, that would finally be the end of free speech in this country?

Bure Valley leper colony continued:

Questions to the Management

1 Why has Bure Valley House got such a bad reputation in the town? Surely, that's one thing you can't blame on me? When the trouble first started and I asked to speak to you about Christine being bullied and abused why did you refuse to speak to me even though you were there when I rang?
2 Do you believe it's true that I have been going around tapping on windows and trying to get into someone's flat at night you assholes?
3 Are there any cameras at Bure Valley House or in the Car Park? How are you always able to know when I am there?
4 How come you know so much about everyone?
5 Its stated that Mrs Didwell handed over sixty of her diaries which contained notes about my behaviour. What is the total number of diaries she has done for you. Could we have them here so we can take a look at the amount of bullshit in some of them please?
6 How many times has Didwell and Freak Temple rang you about me (I was passing her room one day and heard her say she was going to ring you about me being in the garden as soon as you got in Monday morning; "Trust me. I'll lay it on really thick!").
7 Do you *seriously* believe that we openly had sex in the garden or that we have banged repeatedly on the wall for hours?
8 I do apologise for losing my cool when you called at my mother's house with the police to give me the new Injunction. I really let myself down but I am so sick of being hounded by you and by your attempts to embarrass me in front of my new neighbours. As I told you then: the First Injunction was based on lies and I felt you were harassing me even though I left Bure Valley Shithouse months ago.
9 What do you think about 'malicious reporting.' Do you think malicious reporting is a form of 'harassment?' Why have you never done anything to stop this form of harassment?
11 After I moved out in April can you confirm that you threatened me with a hefty fine unless I removed a wardrobe I'd left behind?
12 Why have you never done anything to stop the harassment of Mrs Pigott by her neighbour? What did you do to stop the abuse against her by some of her neighbours? What did you think of some of the slanderous remarks made by people such as Didwell and Temple (SHAP rep) against myself and Mrs Pigott. What did you do to stop them?
13 True or false. You are determined to label me as a nasty dangerous neighbour even though I moved away from BVH months ago. What have you got against me, you two faced two-toned muted skin-head. How are your friends down at the Pig-wagon by the way?

Whispering Woman

When you first moved in what did I do? (*Help her in with her bags. Encourage her to read*).

Who do you think sent those horrible notes when you first moved in?

How did we get along on the coffee morning. Did you enjoy the bingo. What did we talk about? How did we get along. Have I ever threatened or abused you. Have you ever seen me trying to get in your flat or ringing your doorbell or anyone else's late at night? What possible reason could I have for hurting you?

Why did you say that I must have done these things "because it could not have been anyone else?"

You told Christine that you may have been wrong about me?

Reasons for adjournment:

1 I did not receive any official notification from the Court about the Court date.

2 The first I heard of today's hearing was when I opened my post around lunchtime on Friday 20th. It was an envelope from Circle Housing containing a date but no time, and containing the six hundred statements which I already had.

Wherry Housing did this at the first Injunction too. They presented me with the papers a day before the Court case.

3 This gave me little time to organise myself or be fully prepared.

4 A major witness (Mrs Pigott) could not attend this morning because she already had a prior arrangement to look after her grand-daughter. It's very important that she should be here as a lot of the complaints involve her as well.

I spent all day Friday trying to get in touch with the Court:

    (a)   Circle Housing told me the hearing was for ten o'clock on Monday. I informed Circle Housing that I had not received any official notification from the Court about the date.

    (b)   A Court official informed me that some papers had been sent out on October 10th but to my old address. *Wherry Housing have not been in touch with me about them.*

    (c)   The Court should know my new address because it was on the papers I had been asked to send in by November 2nd.

Why should I be placed at a disadvantage just because I am on my own and cannot afford any professional help? I did try to get in touch with the Court as soon as I could to ask for a postponement. It's difficult enough being pushed around by these big organisations who have a lot of time and money at their disposal. I have been experiencing chest pains and shortness of breath. I have seen my doctor about this and several other matters.

Dear Mr Simpson,

Yet again.

I am writing to inform you about the visitors who have been calling every day for the past month. They have been banging on my door. Shouting through me door. Rapping on my letterbox. Calling through my letterbox. Throwing stones up at my window and disturbing my sleep. We go through the same boring routine every time I let them in...

"Let me see now...what have you there...is that your mobile phone? Do you have a smart phone. Is that your laptop. Is that a photo of you. Would you mind if we took a quick look inside your bedroom while we are here. Who is that card from?"

"How is your mum?"

"We know you have been ignoring us. Have you told her yet? It would be a lot better

coming from you. Does she have a laptop of her own?"

"Told her what: that I once contacted my ex partner on the phone five years ago?"

The Boss lolled with her hand on the doorframe. She said that she had nearly a thousand *offenders* like me to boss around on her patch and none of them caused her half so much trouble.

"Don't fuck it up!" she snapped. "Just don't fuck it up here! The Home Office say we have to do it. We are only doing our job. If you keep refusing to let us in we will have to go round to your neighbours and that will all get reported. You could end up back on the streets. Is that what you want?"

"You have been reported for making a noise in the bedroom and for setting off the smoke alarm..."

"Why don't you do one," I said.

"If we have to return with a search warrant there will be four of us and we will break down the door!"

"Do whatever you like," I said. "I still won't be talking to you. I still won't react any differently. It won't get you anywhere."

"We are only doing our duty! We need to know where you are every second of the day."

I said: "leave me alone and stop harassing me. And who invited you to our Housing meeting anyway. Why don't you keep your big fat snouts out of my affairs?"

"I have not committed a crime."

"I have nothing to say to you."

"I am not trying to hide anything."

"Please, just fuck off! If I never saw you again it would be too soon."

She smiled and walked across the room to the sofa. She sat down and started to read my letter.

"If you hadn't done a search on line we would not have had any evidence to get the order."

"All I did was type in her name! My *original offence* was phone contact only. Non malicious, none threatening. Why don't you pick on someone else for a change?"

Webbo smiled. I didn't hug her this time. I didn't want to make her feel accepted. They are not my friends. I don't want anything to do with them.

"We will be coming back for the next ten years while you are on the Register. What's that in the wardrobe?"

"A red alligator with a pipe up its arse!"

Grumblelicker took out his camera and began photographing my binoculars on the windowsill.

He smiled at me. A kind of sorry smile, or perhaps it was a gleam.

I caught his eye on the picture.

"So, you are into young girls now?"

I shrugged. Bluddy smart Alecs.

"You're classed as a *psychopath*. A dangerous Sex fiend!"

"I am leaving to do my laundry," I said.

"We would rather you stayed!"

"Could you tell us who left that sticker on your door about police brutality and who took it down?"

"I could. But I won't," I said.

Webbo looked flustered. She had a huge team of Officers to manage. You could tell. Many did.

I went over to the door: "Please don't steal anything this time. Shut the door too when you leave!"

Last week they were chasing me all over the city. Finally they rang my mother.

"What do you want him for?" she asked.

"We just want to know if he's alright..."

"He was when I saw him last night," she said.

Yes Mr Simpson. This is my life now.

That was a nice suit you were wearing in the paper.

How was the Duke of Edinburgh?

My mum thinks you've lost weight.

Is there an election due?

We haven't seen you up here for a while.

Why did you suggest I write to the Head of Norfolk Constabulary?

Don't you know these people stick together like shite on a shovel.

On Tuesday we were called to the Railway room for the third time this year. Grumblelicker was in the corridor.

"What are you doing here?" I asked.

"Why do you think?" he replied, grinning from ear to ear.

At first Mehmet refused to let me sit next to Christine, then he rescinded. Grumblelicker suddenly appeared through the door and sat down by my side.

"I asked him to come," Mehmet nodded. He's such a little cunt.

"I am not going to sit here with him grinning at me the whole time. I want him to leave."

"This is all about 'labels!'"

Louise smiled.

"You can give the Tosser some feedback later if you have to."

Grumblelicker stood up and opened the door.

"Go away, and don't come back. I am sick to death of you sticking your big fat snout where it isn't wanted!"

Mehmet went through a list of complaints.

He refused to listen to our complaints of slander, bullying and intimidation.

"You set off your smoke alarm in the early hours of the morning!"

"We didn't know how to switch it off. There isn't an extractor fan in the kitchen."

"You made ghost noises on Halloween intending to scare your poor neighbour's grandchild!"

"You set off your neighbour's security light by waving your arms about!"

"I was working late in the garden to clear up the leaves! It goes off as soon as we go out."

"You banged repeatedly on the wall for hours!"

"We have never banged on the wall!"

"Your neighbours could hear you laughing and making love in your bedroom!"

"We have a very healthy and loving relationship. I sometimes tickle her under the arms."

"Mrs. K and Mr B have heard you slam the door repeatedly, and when you were asked to stop you said that Christine could do anything she damn well wanted!"

"I would never say that. No-body can do exactly as they want. I simply said that Christine should be allowed to close her door normally without being harassed. The door was sticking for a time due to the inclement weather. It has been seen to. I haven't talked to Mrs K and Mr B for over a year because they refuse to speak to us and we don't know why. Her son is a serving police officer. I spoke to her about the door over a year ago, when she threatened to take a hatchet to us."

Rosemary's baby

I had been working at the nursing home for six months when the Manager invited me into the office. The Deputy Manager was there too, along with another Carer. On the desk was the daily log. It was open. I was asked to examine my signature in the left hand column and the date.

"We are certain that your handwriting matches the numbers found on top of Rosemary's baby. Was it you?"

"Do you mean the plastic doll which Rosemary holds in her lap in the entrance hall?"

I laboured over my handwriting while the doll was smuggled in.

"We have tried our best, but the ink just will not rub off!"

The doll was thrust before my eyes. It was dressed in white lace and had ginger hair with a ribbon.

"There is a passing resemblance."

"What kind of person would do a thing like that?"

"I have no idea why Rosemary would want to scribble three sixes on the back of her child's head."

Griffin of a thousand days

What became of me,

   when the ground trembled,

and rocked me from my lair,

Into the land,

where Monsters dwelt,

Unto the place,

where wizards went,

Into the hills Moon by Moon.

One tenth of my love spilled like a fountain from the dark,

and banished remorseless time,

With one touch of the dawn.

Beset by mortal winds I cut the tulips from my throat,

Growling and groaning in the wilderness,

like a frozen sunbeam.

The river expanded like a song,

drifting on an upward stream.

A cloud above the earth,

sent yellow fibrils tingling from the sky,

Like a hand sharing its soul to the world,

And,

beating like a Universe of wings.

Dear Local MP,

I am still getting harassed by the police. They came up several times in one week recently even though I have done nothing wrong. I pleaded guilty to contacting my ex partner on the phone five years ago. A short time before the end of my sentence the police applied for a special order and as a result of getting the order were able to place me on the Sex offender's register, even though I had not committed a sexual offence. This gives them the right to ransack my home whenever they wish.

Before I came to live here they went around telling everyone I was a dangerous Sex offender. I have since met a very nice lady who is standing by me but she is being harassed by her next door neighbour for being with me. The *next door neighbour* has accused us of banging on the wall when her grandchild was staying (her son is a serving police officer). We are now being threatened with eviction by Wherry Housing Association who have not bothered to investigate *our* complaints of slander, victimization, and bullying. I have collected twenty signatures testifying to our good character but it's as if they never existed. When I attended the inquiry into the complaint I found out that the Housing Association had invited the police along to the meeting.

My girlfriend keeps asking: "why are they treating us like this when we have done nothing wrong?"

Go on then Mr Simpson. ~Can you tell us?? You say the police are allowed to behave exactly as they like when dealing with socially repugnant individuals. We are trying to get legal aid, but as you may know, it is very difficult to obtain, especially with *that* kind of label. PLEASE DO NOT ADVISE ME TO GET A SOLICITOR AGAIN!

Yours Sincerely,

A Coathanger

Conversations with the Duke of Wellington on the merits of war-medals

Frenchmen, how do you feel...

With your army mowed in the mud,

Your brides turned to gray,

And the Old-guard,

Dashing like nursemaids down the slope?

Worthy of mankind?

The rot of your horseflesh,

   And the rose of your troops,

Plastered in blood...

Le Petit Caporal slavering the mire,

   And the white-boned mist,

   Draping the battlefield.

At the gate

At the gate my heart is rending,
Reaching through the morning clouds,
Sister Mary stands beside me,
Bending down to hold my hand.
Looking through the iron railings,
Wondering if she would return,
The school bell rings, our call to lessons,
As she turns, and walks away.
At the door the teacher beckons,
One whole day, and then to prayers,
When I ran, she stood there waiting,
At the gate, for me to cry.

Monster's Mansion, 4 FEBRUARY 2012

Dear Genevieve, how are you little one?

I hope the inmates on that small island across the sea are treating you kindly…Thankyou for the book you gave me on the myths and legends of Ireland. I am quite familiar with myth building and demonization.

I am focusing on getting my health and strength back. I have just printed up a new story, which I think is a fair account of what happened and why. It was very cold in the city today. I am hoping spring will soon be here. I sometimes go to the marketplace for lunch.

My main problem is money; I don't have any, and you know yourself how far it goes. I saw a pair of trainers for nearly two hundred pounds the other day. I spent Christmas with the homeless up at the church.

It was nice to talk to you on the phone even if it was a bit strained at times. I am really sorry you had to hear such awful rubbish.

I do agree with you that my behaviour was sometimes far below what I consider to be right and proper. It would be very harsh to judge me on what I was then though. I went out with about twenty women in Oxford. I was close friends with a WPC from Southampton and a few backsliders from the Probation dept. Many of my girlfriends have said that they felt protected by me.

If you mean by 'excuses' explanations, then you really have to accept that we all do things because of the situation we are in at the time.

I disagree with you saying that we were never close. We were very close when we were younger. I cried buckets when you left home so there must have been a strong emotional bond. I used to feel it every time we parted and don't say you didn't, because I won't believe you.

You had a cot in the upstairs bedroom. The same one I'd had.

When you got a bit bigger you used to like to climb in and jump up and down. I saw you doing this one day when a terrific plan hatched in my head. I waited until you had gone, and then I climbed in the cot myself and jumped up and down until it smashed the bottom out. Then I ran and brought mum up to show her what you had done.

I am very sorry your friend in the village let you down. You have to choose your friends carefully. If you do tell someone a secret you have to be prepared for it to come out one day. It was something you could have done without though. I don't want you to have any more stress.

I really want you to have a good life. I wonder what John would say. There are people in this world who would sympathise...

I told my story to a lady at the church at Christmas, and when she saw me in town she ran across and put her arms round me!

I watched Great Expectations the other day. A classic film with John Mills, and who is the real hero: Magwitch! You mentioned my needing to live to a strict moral code but you don't say whose moral code you are talking about or where it originated from.

I will always challenge Authority. That is my way.

I can make friends wherever I go, but I will always have a troubled life unless I get very lucky.

I cannot and will not live under these conditions.

Love from your sibling,

Gudrun x

The Death of Superman

We arrived at the hospital just after ten. The nurses were waiting. He was in a special room all on his own. I walked through the door and into the sunlight. He was sitting up in bed looking rather serious. He smiled warmly when he saw me. I couldn't understand why there were so many people. I couldn't understand why he looked so thin, and why a tube was running from his arm.

"When are you coming home?" I said.

Jenny looked puzzled.

The crowd around him remained unusually quiet. I heard one of them mention the newspaper column. He looked at me curiously. Maybe he wanted to say something.

"You saved them all," I said. "How could this happen to you, of all people?"

A lady at the bedside began to cry.

"What about the girl. What happened to the girl. Do you still take her any lillies?"

My mother looked glum. My uncle felt a bit guilty.

She said something to him and fluffed up his pillow.

"The bowls. What shall we do with them?"

I shook my head. Earthly father and mother. One missing.

"You said it was time. You said it was the end of the whites."

He nodded. Like a worn-out Gladiator he lifted his arm.

He motioned towards the grapes on his table.

"If it wasn't for you none of them would even be here."

His hair was peppered with grey, on the steel-like filaments of his head. The square jaw. Now a feeble copy of the man.

Truth, honour, and Justice. The American way. The Big 'C.' We said a prayer.

Jimmy flew in from Canada. Barbara gave up her job. His reading glasses.

Could bend iron bars with his bare hands in the lunchbreak.

"Why did you do it? Why did you try to save such a greedy and self-centred race of creatures?"

I saw him laugh. It was a hollow laugh ringed with tears. 'Not long now,' I thought.

Another Sun. The rocks of Kryptonite eating into his skin.

He turned into an egg cup for newly weds.

Judge McLoughlin

By Bird Dung | Published: January 29, 2016 | Edit

I attended the trial of BUNDERCHOOK today who'd been hauled in front of the Beak for:

setting fire to cars
making people jump or throw themselves
being in a bad mood
tossing a set of keys
having a criminal record
banging on walls all through the night
making love in a neighbour's back garden
staring into a window wanking
Having a red face   sticking his tongue out
URINATING AGAINST A PEDESTRIAN   TAKING THE PISS   PESTERING A MEMBER OF THE CLERGY
SETTING A SMOKE ALARM OFF WHILE RIDING A MOTOR CYCLE

A queue of mutants from the nearby **Bure Valley leper colony** waited at the back of the County Court gleaming like Cheshire cats and stinking like a mile of cuttlefish.

Bunderchook declared his innocence with typical aplomb.

"We must abide by the obtuse conventions of the Law," he retorted, kneeling, bowing and scraping, and picking his nose. Judge McLoughlin appeared irritated and eager for any available choirboy.

"Hurry along there, you wicked fellow! Bunderchook! Do you seriously think I am going to believe a felon like you instead of Fat-arse!"

"But Your Lordship. Even if we did appeal, what's to stop one of your poncy chums from Toff school finding in favour of the lying two-faced twats as well? I might have known you would take *their* side. About the 100mile exclusion zone…"

"Shut your cake-hole at once, or I will have you for contempt!"

"No, I don't like you!" fumed Mr Low. "You have a hairy back and your head looks like chicken-wire."

Judge McLoughlin stood, and was about to disappear…

"You're all a load of intolerant pea-brained cunts," hollered Bunderchook from the back of the Courtroom.

I heard several smart-Alecs close to the front bench gasp in horror.

Judge McLoughlin flinched, and jerked his greying, far too thick sponge of hair.

Bunderchook will no longer be allowed to visit the colony!

Mark my words. Their time will come!

Pass me the bucket someone!

Comments?

Sounds like a complete set up. Typical of the Cronies working for the Establishment who all piss in the same pot anyway. And we all know who is behind it, don't we Mr McLoughlin…How are your friends down at the station?

Sages of the earthly sphere

Ten sages of the earthly plain,
Upon the verdant tree of life,
Each for the rising Sun were born,
At every moonlit bargain.

One wrote of war of war she wrote,
Of battle blood and gore,
The testing which we all endure,
Upon the deal of water.

The second wrote of shame and strife,
Of all the things which shake the boughs,
The third of wine of wine and lust,
At every remnant crossroads.

The fourth of Seas and streams and cusp,
The sage of Five of fire and dust,
The sixth of air and scars and wrath,
And jet-planes in the ether.

The Seventh of hills and church-bell fields,
Of caverns hail and rafter,
The eighth of chills and ancient spells,
And devils in the waiting.

The ninth of mines and wealth and limes,
Of primrose-garden cities,
The tenth of faith of love and hate,
Among the heathen races.

But then I come the sage of Land,
The lord of winds and islands,
The distant bard from worlds above,
From Stars and regions skywards.

Your innocence

QUIETLY,

AND, WITH CRUEL REVERBERATION,

ON THE FOREST PATH OF DOOM,

THE CHOIR SINGS,

OF JEWELS AND FALLEN EMBERS,

DEVOURED BY THE SHADOW'S DEMISE.

NORTHERN LIGHT,

FLUSHED,

BY SHAMELESS INCLEMENCY,

TREADS BY WITH DOWNCAST EYES,

TO SUN-BLEST SKY,

LIKE THE DYING SWAN OF WINTER,

WITH BEAMS SET OVER YOUR SHOULDER.

CHAPERONE GREY,

FLOWERED LIP OF ELISION,

TAKE THIS SMALL TOKEN OF SENTIMENT,

IN BROODING MIST,

EXPIRED FROM YOUR FAULTLESS TENT,

UNBLEMISHED BY A SINGLE CLOUD.

PERVADING WIND,

YOU GLIDE FROM ENDLESS PIERS,

TO LIE CONTENT UPON THE CALM,

THE ICON BLUE,

WOVEN IN A DRIFT OF STARS,

UNTIMELY FROM THAT GILDED DOOR.

"*A typing error in your file!*" yawned Stalker. "It should have read...'delayed a train,' for five minutes. I'll have it rectified at once."

"I advise you to accept their kind proposal!" urged the cantankerous mayor.

"Otherwise it's the sack, and you'll lose all your free travel." Wasn't that the Mason's grip they were both using?

F. considered the body of doctrine with reluctance. It was this final point which finally tipped the scales in their favour.

On his first day at the Terminus the *cider squeezers* searched for any reason they could to send him for an early bath. The *esprit de corps* turned the air blue with their Billingsgate banter.

Under the canopy *Robinson Crusoe* struggled to barber the platform sign as it swung in the Chinook. All good experience for a potential psychiatric nurse. But only F. seemed to realize that Rentagob was really a brown-nose. Gaffer! – hold his head above water...

At the *time capsule* in the distance the supervisor and his staff indulged in personalities as he blushed with obvious embarrassment. Various shades of *Pigmen* crept out of the woodwork during obtenebration it would seem. Tried to 'rise above his station.'

A member of the *S.S.* waited on the tarmac below him. Perhaps there was a cryptic code of practice which he had not twigged just yet. The *Afrikander* stared right through him as if he had just beamed from a foreign continent. He knew better than to force a direct contact with her though.

O'Flanagan had done his level best to block the Flasher's unpopular placement.

When the L.D.C. official had failed to implement his resolution he had corroborated the remainder of the *partisans* to send the deviant straight to Coventry. There was a hideous scar across his southern lip from a drunken brawl outside the *Golden cockerel* decades since.

224

For Sale

Toshiba 28ins colour TV with digibox £30

Clock radio £3

Speaker/Amplifier £8

Binoculars £2

Kodak camera £10

Belkin internet wireless adaptor £5

Mobile phone £3

Mind reading Centipede £40

Assault rifle with telescopic sights £70

Seven sticks of dynamite $50

Six bottles of Cyanide £90

One slightly used Virgin 10p

Shaded dark by moonlight with his misty vision cleared he churned the unremitting labours of his love and jarred against the rigid pearls of her sparkling molars.

With his knee buttressing against her headboard the tiny virgin semblance clenched and unclenched her trapped and griping palm. With the tonne of his maw-worm fagging his pounding heart he forced the hazard stream to scale the heights of sophomore. He urged the pouting mushroom to release the pressure building in his toggle. Great balls of fire. A whitewash.

With his straining pick-a-back becoming numb Grendel uttered the magic words, 'Open Sesame!'

But the incantation whispered so despairingly was without its final charm, and this was no Arabian night.

Her free hand reached up to grip his stem mechanically in her parchment.

Grubbling her taste-buds over their glittering grid, where a glob of syrup wheedled its viscous path into her swallow-hole, sweet Tiffany's eyes opened right on schedule. She issued the penultimate command tickling an eyelash on Old Lugger creamed in saliva.

Her eyebrows considerably narrowed as the tingling sensation began to reach boiling point, and the pumping began like an explosion down the mineshaft, filling her gaping gap with the best of his life-kindling juices, which splashed so abundantly over cheek and jowl.

Remnants of the guzzling flocked her feather pillow as he quickly faded out of sight and lost himself among the globland.

From the nadir of her robes the prowling fiend counted his blessings as sweet Tiffany sat bolt upright in her shorties. She touched her creamy skin where the ambrosia still dripped like molten sugar and began to cough and splutter insults.

Grendel trembled beneath the cliff of the escarpment.

Peering out of focus her hazy indignation snorted a hum of exasperation towards the crouching bundle before settling down once more to slumberland...

183

LITTLE ROBIN **(Natural Surveillance)**

After 'tossing' at the Jorvik he continued to the Shambles, then he retraced his steps towards the capillary of rail intestine, after *mashing beneath the geodesic at Buckminster.*

With his golden plume pinned to the politically correct agenda he became trapped forever in the labyrinth of the skewbald network...

Today the book-shy-blonde dressed in denim was scenting a tattered copy of the *Perfumed Garden* in the traveller's fare.

He ordered a cup of horlicks and sat down at the stanchion.

From the plot he was able to erudite the girl's superb features reflected in the mirror. Though his glance grew like fungus on her two delicious melons she did not at this point vaguely scrutinize his stare.

Her swift blue eyes darted like an arrow in the direction of the loudspeaker...

How he hated hanging about on the filthy platforms. Once he had decided where to blitz there was still the sly invective from the porters as he wandered from pillar to post.

She gazed through the shutter as he strode past her tainted image for the seventh season.

When the 1635 pulled alongside her baggage she flitted agilely through the crowded congress,

Having found a comfortable seat near the door she finished with her *Independent* and carried on with her crossword.

Can you guess who was nervously vellicating opposite? Itching to disrobe and expose his hirsute *rolling-pin.*

The ubiquitous Flash blenched towards the fag-ends each time she raised a friendly glow.

The droiling snore of the commuting dormouse was hardly a distraction so for her eyes only he prepared to play upon his tympan.

He begged to borrow her newspaper — "You're most welcome!"

His swashbuckling penis, luxuriently parted (and blow-dried) with a streak of curly grey...

215

Putting on Emily's shoes

In the morning,

When you rub your eyes,

The door opens,

And mummy calls:

"Hurry, or we'll be late!"

Our jeep lies purring in the driveway.

You sit above me on the stairs,

Your brown hair,

Straight down by your sides,

You look at me,

Without a whisper,

Waiting for something, eating your biscuits.

I try to comb your strands,

But you shake them again, wilfully.

I hunt for your footwear among the bric-a-brac,

The assortment of toys and boxes...

One push and I'm sure it will be alright,

But your tiny feet seem far too big for the space...

So I undo your straps and start once more,

In earnest.

Trying to persuade them in,

Coaxing them along,

And tie them gently.

Now you are free to stand,

And I can swing you up,

High into my arms,

My Sweet Emily.

Burning of the Scarlet Hearts

THE SWIRLING

AT FOUR IN THE MORNING

DEAR CRISTINA

DAVID CARRINGTON-JONES

BUFFING THE GROUND FOR MR TUMBLEDOWN

WALKING AROUND WITH YOUR HAND HELD UP TO YOUR FACE

STRETCHY PULLOVER

THE SUBTLE ARTISTRY OF LOVE

A FAMILY OF ELVES CARRYING MY TREASURE TO THE WORLDS

ONE AGAINST THE MANY

THURSDAYS DARK

RED HAT DAY

RETURN OF THE BLUE CANNONDALE

SWAPPER

FATHER WHY DO YOU BLEED

KISSING THE FACE OF JESUS

ALL THE WORLD

PRIVATE LAND

SMALL BIRDS SING

LITTLE WING

VESTIBULE OF LIGHT

THE WILTING ROSE

RETURN TO FRANZ BIBERKOPF

MY HEART IN THE BRANCHES ABOVE HER

FEAR OF FLYING

DAMP WIRE ON THE WING

MAROONED ON THE RIVER OF HER BED-POST

RIDING A CHARIOT ACROSS THE BAY OF NAPLES

WHAT LITTLE BASTARD

EMERGING FROM THE DRUM OF DEATH'S SHADOW

CARNAGE OF THE FLOWERS

LABELS

CRAZY LITTLE FESTIVAL

SMASHING THE DOOR IN

JACKSON POLLOCK MATRESS

GENERAL APP

SEEING FATHER CHRISTMAS

FALLING LEAVES

DUBLIN WITH THE PIGS UP MY ASS

THROWING BRICKS AT LAMPOSTS

PARALYTIC ON THE DECK OF THE TITANIC

ISLAND OF SINFUL WORDS

RIDING A CHARIOT ACROSS THE BAY OF NAPLES

MASS OF SCARS

THE HUNDRED POUNDS

SECRETS OF THE DEAD SEA SCROLLS

WHISTLER BELIEVES IN FAIRIES

ALWAYS HAPPY

DADDY'S BEST YURT

MY FAMILY ARE MADE OF ROCKS

SEBASTIAN IS CRAZY

IN THE WHITE ROOM

BEHOLD THE GOLDEN COCKROACH

WINGED BIBLE OF THE ASTRONAUTS

SHE NEVER SAILED RUBBER DUCKS

IN THE SHADOWS WHERE I LIVE

MUCKY OLD BURE

HUNTING FOR BOMBSHELLS

FINISH LEWIS HAMILTON

FIRE ENGINE

ALFRED LORD TENNYSON WITH LOTS OF SALT AND VINEGAR

PETER MYSKO

NEIL BEVERIDGE

WITHOUT BLEMISH

BILLY DRESSER'S SISTER

ROMMEL'S BROWING REVOLVER

CREATURES OF LIGHT AND SAND

NOT SO FUNNY NOW

BAFFLING PROOF OF THE SANITARY TOWEL

RED LIGHTS

HELICOPTERS

BURNING OF THE SCARLET HEARTS

HOWEVER BIG YOU GROW

ALL ON LYNCH

ARK OF THE PAGAN

IF YOU REALLY LOVE HER

THE BROKEN HEADED JACKDAW

THE LAUGHING GAUGHAN

FLUFFY

NO KIT FOR FOOTBALL

All-the-world

FROM THE BRUNETTE OF MY PIT,

I SWERVED MY BEVELLED SPINE,

TO FACE THE CURTAIN OF THE FALLS,

TUGGED WITH A DULCET TONE.

WITH RADIANT COLOURS ON MY EYES,

WALKING HAND IN HAND,

I REACHED TO TOUCH THE TINTED GAUZE,

ABSTRACTION IN MY PALMS...

FROM MY CAVE OF NIGHT I FLEW,

AND STEPPED UPON THE GROUND,

THE VALLEY TREMBLED IN MY PATH,

THE WORLD TURNED ROUND AND ROUND.

Across the torrent in one stride,

the tulips far and wide,

I reached to touch the clear blue vault,

before the sky could die.

Around the Sun I chased the Moon,

the earth beneath my wings,

and laid upon the crimson soil,

a nestling of beams.

But when I scuffed upon the land,

ungainly and half-blind,

my golden scales and lizard's tail,

were all that you could find.

Beyond the field of thorn I rose,

near captured in their net,

and sneezed upon the land of Chill,

synged with my loving breath.

If I could tell you all-the-world,

then all the world would know,

If I expired my final breath,

before the cliff of souls....

Private land

A place somewhere,

A tiny patch of soil,

Somewhere you can be yourself,

A little port of moonbeam.

A place where you are free,

a place where you can sit and watch Orion,

somewhere which is home,

A small island in the Gulf Stream.

There is a place I know,

there is a place shining in the distance,

it is a place for you and me,

it is a place called heaven.

Troubadour for the caged nightingale

I'm wondering,

If day by day,

As the notes fall by my window,

There will ever be another ray,

Allowed into this void.

As the shrill grey sky shrouds the unforgiving plain of land,

Bare and bootless,

Untenanted, hollow with a vacant fog.

The whirring Sun,

Glides like a water lily,

Into the creek.

While dying nightly on my steed of silver light.

"Von't somebody help me please?" she pleaded, as her waters burst, and she sunk into unconciousness...

She was haemorraging profusely on the bare floorboards close to death now, which spread around her like a crimson lake, as Danny, propping up the bar in bad company, boasted of his manly prowess before the gruff of his gamesome cronies. Her Silver cross pram conducted its lonely vigil by her side.

Only the auricular organ of the eavesdropper gleaned her empty echo, as the piebald munching grass at the paddy-wagon in the maize above her, jerked his decaying mane, and snorted in annoyance at the raven.

The *hyleg of revelation* ringed to the ankle of Apollo caught fire as he sneezed through a chink in the sublunary sphere.

"Is he dead? Is my baby behind the veil?" asked the wearied young host recovering from her toxaemic coma, as they brought the fruit of her womb bound in the layette already tarred in his own vintage. The vulsella had gashed a furrow in his nut as a welcome to this doltish cabaret.

After her caesarian section the sickly young child with the face of an angel hung on desperately for life.

Clinging to her solitary finger he fastened rarely to the maternal blocks of light.

His luxurient shades fluttered like a Spanish parasol.

"But Mary," sighed Mrs. Ramsbottom, as the widow pryed through the ward.

"He's a bonnie wee laddie! What a pretty baby...surely he must be a little girl? He's certainly got his father's good looks. He's the spitting image of Danny."

6

Riding a chariot across the bay of Naples

I will not ruddy-well wear my shirt inside-out,

nor speak in the cinema out of place,

and I will not put on _little_ boots....

or run naked through the open air,

or talk to who I damn well like.

Wednesday's lecture will be, on why I am so mentally deficient.

You will no doubt explain just where I have been slipping up,

How my abject failure has been due to a mental handicap.

You will tell me that my explanations are simply excuses,

Of course, I am to blame for all the reactions of others.

On Monday I will be back in town, but not to cause a nuisance.

I will not be chased through the shopping arcade for riding my bicycle, and, I will not tease Christopher about a piece of cotton hanging from his cuffs, I will not glue a pound coin to the library floor...even if I had one. Or walk in front of the school bus.

I will not scream at the bloody rain, and turn the air blue, when I hear my neighbour in the garden with her family.

On Saturday I will desist from marching up and down outside the station, chanting and gesticulating wildly.

But when a dry spell is predicted,

and the sun bleaches up from the saltbed,

I will build a bridge-of-barges across the water,

with the wind-blast, and the shimmering,

strap in my horses, to the white white waves,

call on the God of thunder.

Falling leaves

These are the falling leaves I have prayed for,

They are falling from the Sun,

And land like bombshells.

I listen to their frank exchange,

In the garden.

Quiet.

It's all for nothing.

Throwing bricks at lampposts

I went all the way,

from Woodhouse to Utley,

Throwing bricks at lamp-posts,

I knew no better.

It was Jacko and Lynch;

They were my friends then.

My family are made of rocks

My family are made of rocks,

Some are made of dynamite,

They are like old mirrors,

Some are like new slippers.

My family are made of stone,

Wood and stream,

They peel like wallpaper,

Beach-huts seals and lightning.

Some are like skeletons,

Some are like tennis balls,

Dark in the midnight sky,

Covered in rain.

My family are like rocks,

hurled at the face of cliffs,

Like snakes and vampires,

The listening squirrels of angels.

My family are like rocks,

Glistening pieces of salt,

They breed like bloodsuckers,

Over the edge of my dreams.

Burning of the Scarlet Hearts

Like a fleck,

Of shattered Moons,

   Spiraling into Spring,

When true love wanes,

And winter falls again.

Betraying every splendour,

Which you had given then,

My heart was just an ocean,

Which the sky had dipped within.

Bearing every moment,

And every rack of salt,

If you could wet the colours,

And the stars that drip like rose.

Heaven's loyal heartbeat,

words that scorch like ice,

The universe is aching,

With an hour-glass of seed.

Scorching every mountain,

Decaying every bloom,

The places where my thoughts end,

And the lakes which speak of love....

Silver is the colour,

Hands that sprayed with gold,

Spangled with my life blood,

Glowing hearts grown cold.

He paused for breath and adjusted his quare nippers.
"I've been talking to a chick from the homeground who
used to have the low-down with you," he sniggered.
  "Her boyfriend chains her bare arse to the
blistering red hot radiator and screws the hell out of
her! She swears that you were a scruffy little eel at
kindergarten." All shook up!
  "She couldn't believe me when I informed her how
much you had burst at the seams. It's a pity she's no
babe." Vassal miscreant! Edge of the known galaxy.
  "I've had that recurring dream again!"
He giggled just like 'Willie Carson' riding a flea.
  "I dreamt that I was just a shiftless, spineless
Jellyman without any real backbone at all in me... and
that without my complete works of prestidigitation I
wouldn't even appear capable of far-sighted folly, or
voluntary euthanasia. World's so full of shit man."
  But it was always difficult to discern if Bates was
just manoevering one of his many sides, and he had
already rebuked the *hoi polloi* more than once for being
too afraid to fib. Mental detecting. *Boings* were
unemployable! Givers or Takers. Which one are you?

The Cock-or-two repeated his story several times and
offered his 'screwed-up' sketch of 'Lucretia Borgia'
with a penis lodged in its cochlea. Once had a brush
with the law. What's hot on the catwalk Tophat?
  They discussed the gouache water colour which
someone had presented as part of their final
exhibition; a gnostic metaphor containing an *Oran Utan*
being fellated by a member of the 'Tuatha' as it hung
on the cross at Calvary. Only the good die young!
  Underneath its horrid caption, 'Suffer me to come
onto little children;' obviously a biblical allusion
regarding the sacrificial crucifixion and entering into
heaven. *Shunga*...no black without white.
  Its effect on the evangelical movement at the
college had been diabolical. Sins of the flesh! Below
the salt. Must have gone through a fortune in tracing-
paper conscientiously objecting. Defended his
intellectual property throughout.

Here is the letter I've been meaning to send you,
meaning to send you for such a long time now.
I know when you read it, I may be dead...
I may be dead for such a long time now.
But read it, I know that you will one day!

Do you remember when I carried you quite far?
I was loaded with scales but did not think twice,
Oh, what a pretty girl always to me!
I felt very tender, I only felt tender,
and penned the way some porters do...

If ever I hurt you, which I know was not seldom,
then you'd climb and come round with the tide.
From *Whitecastles* I swung you, and sweetly embraced
you, forever I hoped this would be!
But then I grew serious, and you frowned with sad
Autumns, though I should, I never quite understood
why...

But there's something quite often, I meant to beseech
you, which tossed like a leaf in my mind.
Will you quite often, or just for a moment...
will you please *be my bride*,
will you please *be my bride*?

Though I once left you, to shelter your secrets,
and for once march on alone with your cares,
You never quite left me, you never deserted me,
if I could, I'd just like to explain;
I loved you, I love you, I always adored you,
and think of you where ever I glide.

Justice has been done.

"Only jealous!" hissed the Infanta.

The sex object hovered until Zero hour. Her eyes were
rolling mesmerically in and out of consciousness when
he folded his waistcoat as a squab. The *sinuous
serpent of the Nile* crept alongside...his heart soared
like an eagle. Had to hand it to him.
  After verifying her colossal breasts he carefully
tilted his brush-stroke. Lightly testing the livery of
her slip he explored the extent of her opulent fig-
basket. After the horse had bolted.
  Her entry was much smaller than he had imagined, and
her fanny had been recently tonsured. He waved a *green
flag* to bring the patient into contact with his
element. Picture of beauty.
  He positioned the thumb in her mouth and postured
her index up the tweed for an artist's impression. Her
eyes flickered gently open, absorbing his laden grocery
bags, and slipped once more into oblivion.
  It would have been a doddle for him to ejaculate
into the orifice of the *epileptic kissogram-girl*. The
cart was completely free of any gate-crashers. A
slight migraine would have been her only cause for
concern...but just as he was boring an entrance for
some strange reason Old Welshie decided to turn round
on his canvas. Perhaps it was purely instinct.
  The driver's door had blown slightly ajar. He leant
across to stem the draft while keeping a scan on the
advancing track. As he marshalled his architecture W.
happened to glimpse something out of the corner of his
snake. He placed a brick on his handle and leaned out
of the cab to obtain a better picture. Then he
adjusted his mirror as F. splashed about on the swab
deck. Spilling his developing fluid.
  "Holy organisms!" quivered the Flash.
It was precisely at this juncture that the train
accelerated into a tunnel and blew his head clean
off...*Crunch!*
What was so special about a tall dark stranger anyway?

The *mutant* did not bother to check F.'s pass because of
his notoriety. That would save him another space on
the card. Punched her ticket.
  She placed her mut instinctively over her mouth and
panted over his *beef-tongue*. "I thought he was
carrying the *lantern of Diogenes*." So that was her
angle. Thought only step-fathers did things like that.
  Annabelle eventually received the coded message
which was tacitly understood and resolved to mind her
P.'s and Q's. Correct statistical ratio.
  Her friendly repartee gradually evaporated. He
continued to reply in monosyllables. Where was the war
in that? Had the right to a 'proper education.' F.
rose to the occasion and filled his beaming penis above
the tauting balls of lead. He delivered his best shots
in respect of her valour. As the sprigg shone
healthily against the *Aurora Borealis* he teased her
with the bulbous glans which was exposed beyond his
flinching foreskin.
  Her eyes like *Artesian wells* flashed in the
flickering window lens. She pushed the strands of her
hair over the bracelet and veered to loiter on the
radius of his *Druid's Oak* eminently rooted on the edge
of her emeritus.
  Like a duke-box needle in a bottle of dung he
excused the crowds and played a stinker until the
motion could administer opium.
  He lubricated the tip of his finger with a spatula
of saliva and spread the sanies over the spouting
chaps. Banishing all inhibitions to the winds he
unravelled his jar of pickled walnuts and flouted his
hairy caber in view of her Sphinx-like stare. At the
milestone she posed on just the correct wave-length due
to the intensity of light striking her retina.
  She shook her raven hair. The brambles of string
cracked with cannel coal. Her ancient charm with its
outer calm was like a deep lake rippling on the surface
but laced with hidden undercurrents. The 'victim'
peered down the *mouth of the dragon* which opened gently
like a sun-awakened thalamus. Triple whameee!

Walking around with your hand held up to your face

He walked around with his hand held up to his face,

It was so funny,

he had them all in stitches.

His performances made quite an impression on the Masters.

It was his proudest moment.

It was stunning.

A pointless plea to Sidney Whincup

They've buggered up the country yet again,

Is there anyone we can bank-on to be straight?

My cellmate fiddled with his fag,

    The unruly tongue flapping in his mouth,

Declining the dousing of the tap,

He coughed and rattled like a Miner's tub.

"*You will* do it!" she screamed at the older child.

"You will do as you are told at once and switch it off to come and play with me."

Her wide pink lips were prettily covered with fresh make-up as she kneeled between his straddled legs and ordered him to snog the entrance to Paradise.

Suddenly she gobbed in the ashtray.

There was a growl and her eyes sky-dived towards the fracture. She leapt to her feet intending to investigate further. The sun fell in his shoes.

"Who is it?" she called to the terrier. "See if you can find the dirty rotten scoundrel."

I only knew what hunted thought quickened his step and why, he looked upon the garish sky with such a wistful eye. My sunshine, my sweetheart, my rain...

Is there anything you'd like me to do?

"Stand a little out of my Sun!"

Smiled the *Wickerman*.

"I could have been great with someone, and someone could have been great with me."

At regular intervals she tipped her eager spout to moisten her prospering sprigs with her cloudy eyes occasionally watering.

As his penis proudly prodded the late afternoon weather-wise and began to spurt fresh semen on the wind *Griselda* commenced her croon of *Gilbert and Sullivan* at the top of her lungs, and made up her mind never to flinch from the organ of vision. Kojak's revenge!

He fried to a frizzle under the boiling acid. By the time he was due to retire his body was like a blackened bonfire twig...

In the kitchen her *Shout* magazine lay open in its usual place on the sideboard...

Unfaltering in her bond she climbed the stairs to freedom when no concrete answer came.

Below him in the pot was one of Mary's soiled tampons which she had scrupulously omitted to flush.

Every other step she trod Caroline called out anxiously to discern if he was really in the house or just a pussy obnoxious twat.

"Mathew are you there?" she tremoured, as her hand crept over the squeaky bannister rail, mixed with increased suspense and mouth-watering anticipation.

"Hello?" she asked again...standing white faced before the full length mirror.

"Is anybody there? What are you doing now?" Not a word in reply did the deviant utter, as she paused good manneredly before turning the brow...

Her long golden threads began to edge around the wooden surface, above her sultry smile.

Should he let her into his cranny? He was seriously winded.

One more step and she would have a blockbuster to particularize to her peerage.

"Are you there?" she brayed in a weak and yearning tone, awaiting a reply, but none arrived.

Mathew quickly slammed the door shut and began doing up his flies. Too much flare makes a desert.

Thirteen spurts and no 'passes'..."Just like that!"...thank you very much sir!

"Thankyou," she said..."thankyou very much!" she glimmed, winking genially enough to rouse the cockles of his gross infatuation.

But the best laid schemes of mice and men had been known to go astray.

The *tax inspector* turned over her files to begin anew.

It was then that the Fabulous Flash noticed the hideous blain which tarnished the front of his brand-new livery.

He had completed his wayfaring both '*outward*' and '*return*' for the ump'teenth time later that afternoon when he became aware of a reception committee standing by on the station forecourt.

As he dismounted among the other palmers he endeavoured to ignore the belligerant coastguard crouched at the turnkey. Take a dive!

Attempting to appear incognito he deviated towards the *fire escape* which led to his Batmobile.

Shittlegruber earmarked the oddity with the inspired chuff of a Judas goat at the parting of the waves.

Mike Winter tipped his snitch as F. wriggled like a cat at Crufts. Head of the Mafia.

"That's the little prat!" he barked. "He's the egg-head spotted travelling up and down the branchline without any reasonable excuse.".

At the *iron gate* 'Winter' collared him, and read the Wanderer rights. They led F. into the office for an immediate interrogation. He had it bloody coming!

With the bright overhead spotlight radiating in his crystalline lens they demanded to know what he had been doing sight-seeing on the *bug-train*. He WAS sitting in it!

"Harry Ramsdens?" he scoffed. "Your duty pass only permits restricted travel. Let me have a look!"

"So you were visiting the 'Lighthouse' for spare safety-lamps?" taunted the detective.

nettle reed before him, and trying to sting the old man's hand held defensively at his rear.

Eventually they terminated in the drab and dreary works canteen where Shittlegruber attempted to hibernate until hang up.

As he slouched into a half-baked kip he was suddenly awoken by a teabag as it splattered against his lughole. The ruptured contents mingled with the harsh red boils festering on the flange of his withered collar.

It was almost time for the crafty shark to go on extended shore-leave.

Shittlegruber spat like a cornered alley-cat. His stunted neck twitched in a final death-throw as he pleaded for an end to hostilities.

When the Shop-office-man appeared on the scene he seemed like a fish-out-of-water.

Starbuck appeared intent on bearing a grudge over the omission of certain items in his case history.

His words were flung from a frozen glacier.

"Don't you think you should have told them?" he insisted.

"What if they should discover your unfavourable verdict by another route?"

The old fellow was snoring loudly in the cockshut time...

. "Alright! Where's 'Gunga Dinn?'" he sneered, sarcastically. "We have a warrant for his arrest" he joked....There was something about a ladder hidden in the grass.

"H-h-he's up on the roof sunbathing!" responded Shittlegruber; that was the third time he'd been reported in only one week for tanning his organ.

Why orgasm at the end of the street when a free pass meant unheralded freedom up and down the countryside?

Before long F. was on his way to an interview at Rail Lodge.

In a land of loaves and fishes he might be offered a post as *Captain* of the 'Traveller's Fare.'

When I am cold

When I am cold,

Let the screeve-frenzied carrion pick at my bone,

And the many-eyed Woodsman flute with my tongue,

    The Captain drop anchor on the seat of the world,

The Knight with my capture dazzle my soul.

For I am free,

    Of the devils you sow and the darling blue sea,

The ship with my woe.

The joys when you tumbled like a fitful of light,

The fruits that you gathered on the heel of my life.

Except for the lady who must tell how it went,

With a shiver of steel and a shake of her head,

She's putting on costumes like Lady Macbeth,

With a bucket of tears and a titter of mirth....

And yet I must dream,

Of the places I've been,

Standing in puddles on the breath of the Sun,

Warming my hands on the faces I've loved.

Visions

All I have,

Are the mountains I breathe,

The sunrise I shelter,

My eyes are like seas,

The waves they have entered the darkness in caves,

Through a spectrum of leap-years,

From a prism of faiths.

I paint with the contours,

Mould the ceiling with light,

The things that I've met here,

Which have coloured my life.

Over and over the world spins like mad,

Flickering gardens,

With shades good and bad.

Revolving galaxies,

Flying skyward like seeds,

This life was a fine one,

For you and for me.

Seeds of honey

Ju was in the bed next door,

When I heard her moaning:

   Six-months-gone, to my surprise,

   She finished right on cue…

I dropped her at the village hall,

I met her at the station,

And every time we hugged,

I felt,

The warmest sense of loving.

When her arms enfolded me,

And mine replied in tandem,

It felt as if a bird had sung,

And in my heart had landed.

Oleander

Seven years ago,

From Leamington,

You made the journey on the train.

Your lips were like sugar,

Your voice was like honey,

    The prettiest hands I ever did see.

Your skin was like cream,

Your hair like a dream,

    I felt all a shudder when you held me near.

Among the Oxford streets we japed,

    All day long,

    Both hand in hand.

It was a month or so from that,

    We first found a place to share,

    In a four-poster-bed we shared our wine,

    In Norfolk where the ceiling smiled.

Something so sweet,

    Something so sad,

Can hardly find the words to say,

    As if our souls were twined in one,

    For seconds you were my true love.

My true love,

My true love,

    For one short moment life was good,

It felt as if this was the way,

It should have been since I was nine.

Trying to say goodbye

On *Thursday* I will try to say goodbye,

I will leave you,

And go away…

Forgive me,

If I leave a few words scattered around the place,

   Behind my painting hung up next to the fish tank,

   At the back of the drawer,

Or hidden in your handbag…

If I kiss you all goodnight,

As I softly close the door,

And hold your hand before I go.

Here no country

Here no country for my life,

Here no country for a wife,

  No country walk,

  No country stream,

For me to talk,

For me to dream.

No little ones to feed and scrub,

No harvest time to reap my crops,

There are no fruits that I can hold,

For me to raise,

For me to mould.

I am a fugitive by name,

A Stranger on a foreign shore,

The Ferry's sunk, the future's past,

For me to breed for me to plant.

Robin not red

Robin not red,

Robin not red,

You wait by my gate in the summer all day...

  If only you knew how I've waited all year,

For your beautiful singing,

  Your sunshine so clear.

Robin not red,

Robin not red,

You wait by my garden, you wait at the hedge,

Deep in the autumn,

In the willow so near,

There are thieves in the hollow,

   So be careful out there...

You lived through the winter,

You lived through the spring,

And now I still see you right there at the dawn,

 I didn't worry that you wouldn't come,

 I knew you'd be there whatever the clime...

As you fly from the branches and you hop down the path,

 I am still waiting for you at my step...

We talk at the window,

We talk on the stairs,

Forever I pray,

  With you in my eyes…

For I couldn't tell you how different you are,

  If ever you faded,

    My life would be gone…

Robin not red,

Robin not red,

You wait by my gate in the summer all day,

    If only you knew how I've waited all year,

For your beautiful music,

    Your sunshine so dear.

Saving the cream of milk-bottle tops

On the doorstep,
Standing still,
The burrowing of birds,
In the winter chill.

I kept only reds:
For what imaginary purpose you may ask…

To glitter like a round of worlds,
I gave my mother one of those.

Crossing the line

We were a motley band of half-wits,

Frog collectors of every kind,

Sprogs with runny noses,

Who knew no better,

Than to climb the fence,

Ripping our clothing,

Tossing rocks and sleepers,

Debris upon the tracks...

With our can of worms,

And our carts of loving girls,

Our tales of daring,

Excreting on the warning signs,

In a quest for blackberries,

Cutting across the yellow-belly line,

Treading the ladder of dust and bricks,

The tingle of impending doom...

Poised upon the silver head,

Our arms outstretched,

The far-off chuff of steam,

Pistons shoving back-and-forth,

The signal arm leaping off,

We dashed like clowns across,

Chased by a ribbon of flame,

And all our bridges left behind.

She noctambulated him plodding back to his filth for the second confuncture. He helped himself to the residue of gulp having given up the ghost...

"Look at the beautiful scenery you've been missing," he diced. "The sway is like *Quicksilver* and the sky is like silk." With Canute's hands to whip up a storm.

But she hardly spoke another word. Was it something she had consumed or had he put the cart before the horse? Played left-back for England!

After tracing Pisa he deserted the empty compartment and deviated down the catenation to condone his compulsive habit. Unable to forage in palladium he fell into a deep slumber upon the bench.

Suddenly there was a gust of cold wind. The door blew open in an avalanche. Grenadiering in the gap tottered a slimey creature from the hills.

The lofty 'Mountain man' was dressed in a kilt of Yeti skin trimmed with fur gaskins.

A horrid stench rattled from wall to wall as he slid the screen across the passage...

F. woke to find the brute stretched across the other side. Flames of the window above me.

As he quickly gathered his belongings the Darkman seemed to floe his breath.

F. redeemed himself another quod at the front of the plummeting tumbrel.

It was daylight as they trammelled through the overcast countryside when the lid of the compartment drifted wide once again.

A giant hoof stepped inside the room and found a seat crushed in the middle of Tuscany.

Rubbing his grumbling abdomen the leviathan began lacerating an enormous can of corned beef with a penknife from his rucksack.

Sweat was pouring from his ruddy flesh and a pungent odour permeated from his guts as he chomped his cob of bread in syncopation. His soporific globs seemed to barm into viscous broth.

One traveller actually held a scarf to their nose. A local woman muttered disagreeably. He grunted a brief reply in a voice which was *just as awful*.

244

"One autumn festival I was in my room fast asleep when I woke up to find an enormous shape hovering above me..."

"My dad said, 'it'll be him!'. What do you think it could have been?" She shuffled her feet and prepared to draw her own conclusions. Flagrant abuse of power and privilege.

Could have called for the batmobile.
The lodger was polaxed for a second. His lips turned chalk white. Sitting on pins-and-needles.

"Perhaps it was the specter of your recently departed, dear old grandfather?" he answered.

Mathew belvedered for signs of open rebellion...he scrawled 'Wangled' across her maths homework.

On the jaded road below traffic flowed like a mysterious mutant army as he turned his head for what he vowed would have to be the penultimate injection of the radio-active wonder serum.

His bloodshot eyes rolled towards the roast insensible of all consequence on the banquetting cloth as he removed his bleeding biretta.

A flock of inquiring sycamore fell from the russet eaves above and floated by the window of the White room as the stealthy steganographer admired the X-ray photograph by the ebbing phosphor of Selene's silver lamp.

Like a repugnant gargoyle he flew in a flailing motion over to her bedevilled frame. The glitter of his discordant image appeared from the grey of his separate double life.

With a sickly grin spreading beneath the unturfed thatch from ear to ear he contemplated the tender excesses of his composition and began ringing the chimes of the 'Moonlight sonata Interfada.'

"You will!" he stated with expert venom. "You must!" he warned her vehemently with extra tocsin.

The single entity perching desolately on her naked reef prepared to meet the perspiring late night stalker shivering catastrophically.

190

BODGER

My heart in the branches above her

When we set out on our pathway,

from the gate, up Garden Lane,

there were three words from my pillow,

which were tagged on to my sleeve.

If our teacher, is not looking,

I will reach for her left hand,

though I dare not, it would shock her,

and my secret would be found.

On our journey to the Castle,

we were chirping in the spring,

past the ivy and the fountains,

through the sunshine and dark trees,

by the hours and the flowers,

along the cages and the birds,

her smile was like a raindrop,

which had glittered down to earth.

There's an aching in the branches,

there's a trembling in the air,

a piercing cry of sadness,

if I seek but she's not there.

Waving from the tree-top,

   hidden by a bough,

      my little voice is calling,

         but soon I'll have to go.

As you wind along your pathway,

through the crowds of yester-year,

know the heavens, they are weeping,

for a soul I love so dear.

When you've stopped your chiding,

and your scolding melts away,

look high, into the branches,

for the truth is still up there...

☆ 'It's the savage beatings when he flits home every night, to a hair's breadth of his life...he's not her husband's son, he's not her husband's son!'

So at sixteen, and flushed with wanderlust, dharma's lamb grew ready on the boat...to Albion, land of 'hope and luck,' recovering fresh from war, Danny kissed the ring-prowed ship. Rising on the surf the churning deep corbeau reflected in Danny's boyish eyes the seagulled sky of perse...

Nomarchy and toparchy, and occasionally shire took him in, where yes, Eire's greenhorn youth sowed a few wild oats on the foreign soil.

For seven long years while her sore vexed dial at the window often prayed they never received a line.

Until the season when the 'Embassy' telegram confirmed the seventh son had not foundered as they feared.

Near the bank where the *buckled river* rushed, the vital textile centre and *Hall of luddite fame*, where Danny's dandy duds made him stand out in the crowd, at the Mechanics Institute Ball.

In the dowdy shanks of threshold with his finger in the pie...well, it must have come from somewhere, and she hadn't been bathing in the spout before his idle moment of pleasure.

Virgin birth, immaculate misconception! How, how trust a heathen's word? But 'our' Danny's always been a gentleman; he'll do the honourable thing.

Impregnated by a single drop and her hymen still intact the daughter of Eva blushed with pride at being married to 'the handsomest man in town!'

Immaculately dressed, the happy couple emerged from their inaugural orifice to confetti in their locks of wool. He weighed his oars. Shy little mill girl. Trainee midwife. See how the land lies.

Didn't even know about the facts of life.
'Now that you've made your bed you can lie in it!'
Shall we remove the fig-leaf to make them conscious of their nakedness?

2

The Big-hand

You could be just sitting there,

Minding your own business,

Or eating fish-and chips...

It could happen any day,

But usually just after *closing time*.

You could be just standing there looking out of the window,

When the Big-hand appeared,

Taking you by surprise.

That was the main thing.

It could strike from either the right, or the left,

So you always had to be on your toes.

Brought along in handcuffs

I was seated in my chair,

Under the yellow spotlight,

   Listening to their stares,

      Keeping an eye on their voices,

With the tape-recorder running,

And interrogated about *chocolate*,

About the Quality Street,

   Found in her coat pocket,

Which she'd handed round to friends.

Longer sentences for men

By Sarin | Published: October 3, 2014 | Edit

Why do men always get the blame and end up with longer sentences than women; in many cases the woman gets off and the man goes to prison: take the recent case of Sam Tree and his wife: I have even heard of a woman stabbing her husband to death when he came home, only to receive a suspended sentence because she claimed he abused her? Praise be the Lord!

Women never lie of course.

EXTREMISM PREVENTION

By Surloin Steak | Published: September 30, 2014 | Edit

Yet more laws are on the way in the UK which will further curtail our liberty and freedom of speech. It won't be long until *this* Home Secretary will have you imprisoned for voicing any opinion which is different to her own. It doesn't matter whether your opinion is linked to terrorism or not, as long as it is perceived as 'dangerous, different, or perverse.' Theresa May *may* have proved at last that the British police force are not to be trusted, but who is going to say which viewpoint is extremist. The Archbishop of Canterbury, perhaps, or just some creep working for MI5? Their task will be to IDENTIFY, CHALLENGE, and DEFEAT, any view which is seen as a threat. Opinions vary as to how this will be achieved. Some advisors stress that a new form of **'banning order'** could be introduced. Other influential people close to the Prime Minister are saying it is best just to throw anyone they don't like the look of straight into jail….I presume this will mean more dawn raids and the authorities pilfering through everyone's private belongings in the hope of finding an illegal plan. This, of course, is not seen as at all extremist by those dictating the rules.

Internet troll

By Usuli Twelves | Published: October 6, 2014 | Edit

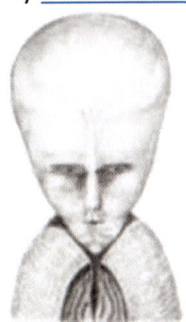

Internet trolls are poor lonely individuals without two cents to rub together or a single friend in the world. They have no right to express an opinion and should be chained to their own bog rail. However…! I am still campaigning for a list of Judges, MP's and public servants to be posted on the Internet with their current addresses and their actual area of expertise. I would like to know EXACTLY what qualifications a Judge, Bishop or Member of Parliament has which makes them think they know better than everyone else.

I claim the right to be as obnoxious and vindictive as any tabloid journalist. I reserve the right to be as provocative and disagreeable as I like. False rumours will be my escutcheon! I will ask the most awkward questions I can without fear of compromise and when I've finished putting the boot in I will disappear back into the woodwork or under the stone from which I crawled. *No comment?*

Why we wear the veil

By Sarin | Published: October 3, 2014 | Edit

We wear the veil to protect our skin from sunlight and dust particles. It's to protect our tender bodies. The beauty of our skin should only be glimpsed by our partners. Nakedness is evil! So are surveillance cameras...

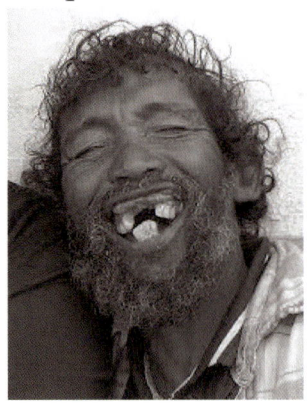

Just like Bobby Charlton

Likened to a man of trust,

A man who always did his best,

Who played with all the love he had,

A kind man, and a Champion.

Catching sounds for Mrs. Hodgekiss

Cars in a hurry on the road,

Pigeons cooing on the nearby ledge,

   Lessons farther down,

  And the boom of bands,

   Playing in the town.

The creaking of our chairs,

Heels rocketing the hall,

The thud of firearms,

   Up on Highfield farm.

Our squeaking pens,

Pram-wheels on the cobbled lanes,

Mothers weeping on their own…

The purr of Lucy on my lap,

The froth of Guinness in the hearth,

Signal-levers skimming in the frame,

I cup my hands,

And travel back again…

Adam's tree

In a corner of the garden,

Beneath the rightful tree,

He's sitting with his album,

Looking seriously.

It is summer in the city,

But here it's always kind,

Below the swaying branches,

And their canopy of leaves.

Slowly through the pictures,

With a deep and broody frown,

Then suddenly he's smiling,

Sending forth a scream.

I wonder what he's thinking,

As he turns another page,

Holidays at Henfryn,

Or a visit to the Barn…?

You can almost hear it breathing,

That old and trusty bench,

Stretching through the shadows,

And holding still the cards.

Supposing that I told you,

There's a lesson for us all:

How families stick together,

And manage through the Fall.

How Adam's tree is shining,

Through the caverns of the dark,

Like a candle in your bedroom,

Or a praying in your heart.

The way it should be done now,

Steadfast, true and firm,

Suddenly he's missing,

But his love is here to stay.

The pit-falls of peeling onions

Dark and wet,

The evening as we sailed,

The hiss of lamps like vigilante birds.

For hours did I sit,

Four hours I stayed,

Glued to the chair and wordless.

"Carefully!" he said.

"Let me hear it once again.

Make sure you have it right my son."

At last we made it to the gate,

The gleam of rain-soaked windows,

 in the street.

Flying Geography book

According to my limited knowledge of aircraft,

Books, were never meant to take-off.

They were never fitted with passenger seats,

Or propellers of any kind.

They did not have a bomb-deck,

Or wheels to make them land better.

Geography books did not start out,

As weapons, designed,

To flap over the heads of pupils.

Boring old cigarette-lighter

It's an old story I know that,

About a tarnished little box,

  The villain of the piece,

In the foyer,

Where the Drinkers gathered.

A mosaic of dancing girls,

Like pass-the-parcel…

Now you see it, now you don't!

Plumes of claret wind,

Growing larger,

Hoots of laughter.

I stooped over,

  And shuddered,

And said goodbye,

To my long dark lashes, forever.

Busy bodies

By Godfrey Winklebacker | Published: March 13, 2015 | Edit

The **history of mankind** is full of interfering do-gooders, intent on telling us all what to do, and obsessed with the need to clean up the world and make it 'better.' Comments

Farage makes cock-up

By Adumla | Published: March 12, 2015 | Edit

The UKIP leader was severely criticized today by Prime-Minister David Cameron, who said: "I find his comments extremely disturbing."

Mr Farage had drawn attention to outdated employment and racial legislation.   It seems that any statements the UKIP leader makes on any other subject except race are outlawed by the press. I suppose this kind of demonization is to be expected from a Prime Minister who is prepared to jump on any popularity band-wagon and who is happy to turn the country into a police state. As Mr Farage once said: "I don't trust a single word he says."

Don't try to bullshit *me* again Mr Cameron!

Okay for British to fight in the Middle East

By Adumla | Published: March 12, 2015 | Edit

It's official. You are alright to fight in the Middle East, and to travel on British Airways, just so long as you are fighting on the *right side!*

A mercenary from Britain said:

"The terrorists don't wear uniforms. We wear uniforms, therefore we aren't terrorists."

He also added: "I was *compelled* to do it!"

With logic like that it's easy to see how the British colonized the world.

Rich boy gets away with murder

By Sarin | Published: September 12, 2014 | Edit

I can't help feeling that it's 'who you know' in this life. If the defendant had been poor then a life sentence would have been a formality. But then he wouldn't have been living in a penthouse which looked more like a celled fortress. I heard the other day about a guy being sent to jail for taking some golf balls which had fallen in the pool at the end of the course. They're having a bloody laugh, aren't they? He was obviously not the son of a 'Judge' or a member of their selective little club then…

The right to bare arms

By <u>Usuli Twelves</u> | Published: September 8, 2014 | <u>Edit</u>

Readers of the Guardian are frequently moaning about the lack of restrictions in the U.S. It's usually after some oppressed and miserable individual takes their revenge on society.

I think it's about time we reconnected with our past and reclaimed this essential right.

Are you with me?

Life on other planets

By Lawrence van Der Splurgen | Published: September 24, 2014 | Edit

I know why God decided to destroy life on Mars. He didn't want the bacteria developing into new more irritating forms of life.

LANDRU'S LAMENT

By Rumplestiltskin | Published: September 23, 2014 | Edit

We lament the passing of James T Kirk as Captain of the SS Enterprise. His brave and bloody fights against aliens on other planets will never be forgotten…

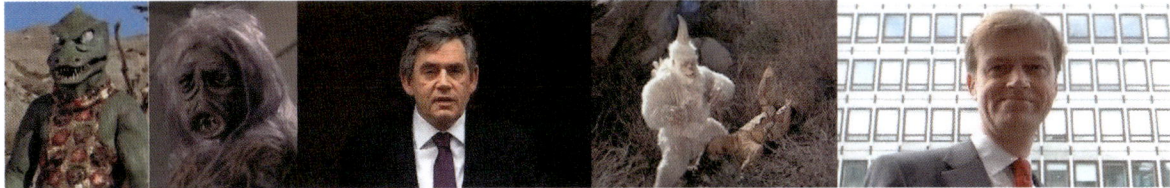

PISS BUCKET

When you get home from school this is what you find waiting in the kitchen: a woman perched over the plastic shell of a bucket with the handle covered in piss and the sound of urine hitting the throat.

The best

By Lawrence van Der Splurgen | Published: September 30, 2014 | Edit

Jimi Hendrix Rory Gallagher Peter Green

Reckless by name...

By Usuli Twelves | Published: September 28, 2014 | Edit

FORWARD TOGETHER

 A lot of Tory MP's and hangers-on are moaning about another rash infraction to UKIP. They complain that Mark Reckless has been disloyal, dishonest, and above all *selfish*. Please, will someone tell me, what MP isn't?

MP sent sex messages

By Usuli Twelves | Published: September 28, 2014 | Edit

So what!

George Clooney wedding dress

By Usuli Twelves | Published: September 28, 2014 | Edit

Quite honestly, I don't give a flying turnip what they were wearing, what they were drinking, and what frigging fashion accessory they had on their boat trip. Does anybody?

Mr President

By Surloin Steak | Published: September 27, 2014 | Edit

Please remember: on your next mission to *gather intelligence*: It's okay to go to war. Just so long as you are a Christian. ***We'll never give in to terrorism!***

The day I met Clint Eastwood

It wasn't very wise,

  To be just standing there,

In a cold Oxford street,

  When I should have been working.

But eventually he arrived,

  In a dark limousine…

As he stepped from the motor and walked towards me,

  With his escort…

I held out my hand ready with:

  "Do you feel lucky punk…"

"Well do ya?"

Held accountable for blushing

If it were a sin,

then I would walk on hot coals forever,

passing each cloud,

as if it were a seething spring.

Shunning each intimate moment,

Steering clear from every place,

where people dwell.

Seeing each hall,

as if it were a Court of law,

harming every sunlit waterfall,

  and haven.

Missing Demis Roussos?

I don't miss him at all really.

Dear Job Centre,

I recently joined a gym and was getting on quite well. I even designed a poster for them. It's a Community gym filled with local people.

I was soon offered a job with them as a qualified Instructor but just the other day a chap walked in who recognised me from *the Bure Valley Zoo.*

Since then everyone has started cancelling their membership...

DANNY

How now my *Diaeneces*! It's a fine April morning, don't
you agree? Why not remove your mantle and settle
with me for a while on this charming knap of rising
ground; as we glance through that sparkling partition
of leaves at the beginnings, among the synged wade of
once proud buckwheat where the yellow sun shines, and
beyond where the cottages are still smoking.

Do you see him?...there!...there where the tall
Cathedral stares, under the sleeping shadow of the
Mountain's of Mourne. Like a carrier pigeon he floats
through the ramage as Dagda supines plucking on his harp.

And now he's hopping over stepping-stones on the wind
tunnel from the barn. Swinging on the chute he's given
them the slip dearheart. In the Apple tree he climbs
filled with virgin blossom, and that infectious grin of
his. He's so full of mischievous laughter!

Scattered like dust his procession of petals
embellish the emerald carpet below. Look at his bright
blue eyes as the nimbus clouds drift across the heavens.

'Do you think he's over the moon?'
'Now that the school inspectors have hauled down the
 flag!'
'Do you think he'll ever learn?'
'Perhaps that time will come!'
'Maybe he'll return with the rain?'
'Perhaps they don't give a dam.'
'Oh! Daniel Pierce, your mother's favourite child, why
are you always playing down on Brady's farm?'
Or submerged in the sike at Red-Dan's place of rest...

'The ambience will invigorate him; he's *Swallowed the
Golden Sun!* Though the illness did him harm, they say
that now his head is cured.'
'But doesn't he desire to lap by mammy's warm
fireside in the heimal after spring?'

A SIGN OF THE TIMES

Hi! My name is Felix Liquorice, and I'm the son-of-the-Antichrist, at least, that is what they say. In the middle of a troubled relationship with a local Health Visitor, who ran a clinic on 'sexual health' in her spare time, I had been getting changed in a clothes shop, when a female assistant saw me partly clothed, as she passed a garment through the curtains. Since then I've had my life turned up-side down, and suffered interrogation after interrogation about my motives. I was forced to attend a programme for serious Sex-fiends by my 'Treatment Manager,' and ordered to inform my employer, and anyone else connected with me. I was arrested three weeks after the incident by four burly police-officers and dragged through the crowded shopping precinct down to the nearest drubbing-Centre in handcuffs, where I spent ten hours in a police cell waiting to be told what would happen. My partner had begun drinking heavily and suspected something was wrong, but I just couldn't bring myself to tell her…I rang my employers to tell them I would be late home. I was looking after their son, who was disabled. I said that I sometimes felt as if no-one loved me…

I first came to Abingdon in 1997, when I was looking after a retired Royal Engineer in the area. We used to drive each day around the Oxfordshire countryside and often stopped to wander around Sutton Courtenay churchyard, or had our dinner in the pub nearby. Sadly, he died a few years ago, and had been suffering from Parkinson's. My history teacher at St Blade's Grammar school once said that I was 'Oxbridge' material. I never got to the University Mr Moore (although it wasn't because I lacked the ability), but I did manage to find my way there eventually.

I was dating a Senior Probation Officer close-by, who I had met on the train coming down from Leamington Spa. On our first meeting we walked hand in hand through the streets all day and when we split up I slept with her photo under my pillow for over a year.

She had a thing about fidelity and always telling the truth. I thought we shared a lot in common…until I discovered she had gone with an ex boyfriend the week before we travelled to Florence.

I began working for a reputable academic family in the area looking after their son, and was very proud of the work I did. I even learnt to teach 'sign-language' as part of my job, and became a 'Friend of Creation,' a local performing arts group. I really enjoyed caring for someone. During my stay in Oxford I made a lot of friends, and enjoyed a variety of experiences. As a boy I'd been a keen reader of *CS Lewis* so it was an honour to meet some of his old Associates.

Even though my Health Visitor encouraged me to move in with her I was never totally comfortable, but I tried my best to fill the place of her husband who had walked out on her. I thought that it would help her a lot if we behaved like a real family. We even attended her local church together, where she was learning to play the violin.

"You'll never give up your job to be with me!" she complained.

It was only later that I discovered she was taking 'Prozac.'

Over the eight months we were together I was constantly searching to understand her better, but she changed her mind more times than wind changes direction. She asked me to marry her, but I said it was too soon. I wasn't sleeping too well, but I still looked forward to reading her two young children their bedtime stories, and carried them sleeping in my arms gently to their bed each night. I never got to finish the *'Magician's Nephew.'* One of my own favourites. They seemed a bit spoilt when I first met them, but I soon grew to love them both and would never have done a single thing to hurt them.

She dumped me by text message on the morning of my Court appearance, and said she *didn't know me*…the *most* hurtful thing she ever said.

"I had sex with three different men while you were away this week!"

Those words were still left ringing in my ears.

Although I went on to meet with other people, I just couldn't forget the closeness we had shared and I guess I had bonded with her two young ones. I missed the intimacy of a close family life. I sent her the occasional text: I still love you

   I miss you

Back would come the inevitable response:

   'Fu.k off, you impotent loser!' or,

   'Get lost, or u r nicked!'

Most people would have given up right then and there.

I guess I must be a glutton for punishment, meeting all these crazy people.

I've never really known when to quit.

I recall her saying when we met:

     "Do you think you could love me, just a little bit?"

     "You don't really love me do you, I can tell?

"Two seconds!"

Her kids were always getting ready for bed, or kicking off.

I felt she needed someone to look after her and give her some support, but there were times when I walked towards the door and she chased after me. I know I've done some very stupid things in my time, but going to her home uninvited was very risky, even if it was only to sit with the cat purring greedily on my knee and wetting my leg. It wasn't really an excuse: still having my property in the house, and having a key…I even left my favourite *Taste* compilation in her stack. It has even been suggested that I was becoming a little 'obsessed.' I needed something to occupy my mind.

I sent her father, a Professor of Literature, a copy of my latest book of poetry, which contained something about his daughter, and a poem written in Polish, just for Lydia. I kept a diary, but only logged anything I thought was funny.

In March 2007 her son saw me leaving the house and locking the door behind me.

Even though there were two sets of lodgers and their friends, constantly coming and going from the house, I suppose it must have scared him after so long. *I remember my own father waiting outside where we lived for ages. We were frightened. I should have remembered. My father was at times a violent alcoholic and had tried to take his own life while I was still only a schoolboy.*

In the morning the police raided my holiday home, and found a Browning semi-automatic revolver, and some rounds of ammunition, included so-called *dum-dum* bullets. They also found my ceremonial dagger, a bottle of Chloroform which I said was for killing rats, a piece of skipping rope, and some duck-tape (which I used for my bicycle). A small amount of cannabis I'd experimented with still went on the charge sheet.   I was always the one to make the 'stink-bombs.' They asked me about an old pair of knickers. Had I ever worn them? A very strange question to ask in my opinion.

I rang my mum from the police station to tell her I was going to die in prison. That is what I thought.
My step-father wanted to know what on earth I was doing with a thing like that!?
The police wanted to know what the tablets were for…
They even turned up in prison to ask me about some *Quality Street chocolates*, which they had found in my ex's coat pocket…and there was I thinking it wasn't a crime!
The following few months were a living night-mare.
If there 'is' a hell-on-earth, its name is '*Bullingdon!*'
"Have you ever been sectioned, Liquorice?"
"Not that I'm aware of!"
The three Officers stood over me were in hysterics.
"I'll have you shipped out of here so fast your feet won't touch the ground!" she smirked.
Every day I woke up made me wish my gun had actually worked. They told me I would get a year inside for every round of ammunition, and by that time the police had bumped up the number to thirty.

Fortunately, the friends I had made in Oxford stood by me and kept on saying that I 'had a future.'
The Officers played tricks on me every day. I was given a 'behaviour warning' and segregated in a cell on my own for wearing the wrong colour pants at lunch. For the first time in my life I began suffering from claustrophobia. I was determined not to take the anti-depressants proscribed for me though, as I could see the effects all around me, and could only feel pity for the many young men who slashed their arms or threw themselves over the balcony. It was an alien world I just couldn't countenance. There was one black guy I knew who eventually tried to set fire to his cell because they wouldn't leave him alone. Prison gave me plenty of time to reflect on what caused me to be there.

My meeting with my childhood sweetheart Lydia. My inability to satisfy her demands. My letters charred and burnt, returned to me in the post. The cosmetic surgery. And Mary.

I had another migraine headache one night at two in the morning. My cell-mate was still dancing round the cell, with the music blaring. I had been assigned to do 'penny-washing' at work early the next day.

"Haven't you ever worked?" I asked him.

Sure he nodded; "I used to be a dancer in a gay nightclub."

When I appeared at the Crown Court the Prosecution tried to make me sound far worse than I actually am, but that is what they are good at. As Melanie used to say, "We all have problems, Felix, just different ones."

The Judge wisely listened to both sides, and read my character references. My Barrister said that it was a unique case and asked for the most lenient sentence possible. He had an eye-patch which made him look like a Victorian money-launderer. I still received a prison-term of two years though. My sister Grendela flew over from Ireland to see me, and promptly burst into tears. I wish I'd been there more for her. I saw the *gleaming spires*, but it was from the inside of a prison van, among the sunny streets, and glimpses of places I once knew flying on my shopping rounds. It would be a long time before I could cycle on my *Stump Jumper* again. My artwork was being examined for any signs of subversion. Travelling in that bus to court and back must be the lowest point of life, I have no doubt. It was weird seeing those familiar streets from inside a tiny cell. ***I was always handcuffed***.

As I was approaching the end of my sentence I was walking down the corridor to dinner with my plates in my hand when a man attacked me suddenly from behind and began punching me repeatedly in my face. Before I knew it I was covered in blood and we were slipping all over the corridor. During the whole attack I never once retaliated. Even when I managed to hold him down in a doorway and call for help he was still trying to bite through my clothing.

The man was a violent psychopath, serving a long prison sentence for rape. He said I owed him a Mars bars...I asked for the police to be brought in. He was given a 'police caution...' I nearly passed out. When I appeared at the food hatch in the morning the Officers made fun of my appearance...

"And how is our resident Panda?"

I asked the art-teacher for some picture varnish.

'"What on earth do you need varnish for, Mr. Liquorice?"

I left prison in March 2008. I can't say I aren't glad to see the back of it. I'm now in a 'bail-hostel' where they watch you night and day. There are cameras in every room, bars on all the windows, and they say you can get recalled to prison for *breaking wind in church*. It's part of my 'rehabilitation,' and reintegration into the community. My father died a long time ago, and his membership of *Sinn Fein* elapsed with him, but he would have been terribly shocked by what I've been through. I have to report every hour to the desk here, and if I am so much as two or three minutes late I have been warned the police will be called, and I will be recalled immediately to prison. I'm forbidden to enter a 'Wimpy' bar, or even a library. I am not allowed to make any new friends unless 'they' have been round there first to 'warn' them all about me...I've been strictly advised never to join any Naturist club. My sleeping tablets are kept under lock and key. I can't even go to the bank, without having a *Tracker* stood over me in case I do a 'Lady Godiver.'
My 'Offender Manager' says that I am classed as a 'Very-high-risk.'
The only ones *I've* heard of who are considered *low* are buried in the cemetery.

They are glad to hear I have decided to do what most people do *these days*, and that is *move on*, and forget...I don't think I'll ever come to terms with the way people say they love you dearly one minute, and the next they have hopped into bed with someone else though...but 'moving on' is the one thing I aren't allowed to do.

I won't be going back to Oxfordshire for some time, having done my time, as it forms part of my 'exclusion zone.' That, and parts of 'Wales.' They spent six hours yesterday hunting through some film-footage just to prove I *had two slices* of toast for breakfast.

There has to be a better life somewhere in existence.
If memory serves me correct, the sign for 'Go-now' is a forward waft of the hand, and a finger pointed directly on top of the wrist.

The Map

One of the most pleasurable things in life for me, at the tender age of 51, is to cycle through the splendid Oxfordshire countryside, a pleasure alas, which has been forbidden me.

I was initially told that my stay at the hostel would only be for a short time. Now I'm told it could last for many months, and that they could almost keep me here indefinitely, especially if I get caught with a leaflet for an 'Indian head-massage' in my bedroom again.

Left alone with a female under such relaxing conditions may suddenly release all my pent-up emotions, and my towel may even slip from its appointed place. Was I a *control freak,* they asked?

Today I was told that I would not be able to cycle anywhere when I return to Norfolk owing to my risk to children, and the fact that I might unwittingly flash at someone on my travels.

A health and safety inspection of my room uncovered an illicit *map of the Chilterns*: I was immediately hauled in front of the police to explain its significance.

Owing to my obvious danger to society I am discussed at monthly meetings of 'MAPA,' a multi-agency big-brother surveillance team, who monitor people like me for the good of the general public. I've been told they might even put a SOPO on me, which basically means they can do what the hell they like with you for life. I still keep telling them I was depressed and that I didn't intend to hurt any other person, but no-one takes a blind bit of notice, and they just write what the devil they like.

I think that when life gets so bad you don't want to go on you should be able to go to your doctor for a 'happy' pill, and end your life with dignity, but what interfering busy-body is going to agree to that in this day and age??

With regard to the *second* Statement of Mrs Didwell (2015)

(Clause 3) I have never intentionally caused Mrs Didwell or her husband distress. This statement is a repetition of a previous statement. According to our information Mrs Didwell was going around telling everyone she was going to get rid of us both long ago.

As I have already mentioned elsewhere: Mrs Didwell was reporting my friend Christine and other people at the home she didn't like even before I came to live there.

(Clause 5) I have not deliberately caused a nuisance to anyone at Bure Valley House. For a period of over a year I successfully ran a bingo and coffee morning for some of the older Residents, against much opposition from Mrs Didwell and her friend Mrs Temple who had previously ran it.

(Clause 6) I have not caused any noise nuisance to anyone at Bure Valley House and I do not believe that Mrs Didwell has filled something like nine diaries with incidents of my anti-social behaviour.

Paragraph 2: I was not there but home in bed at 4.20 am. I did not say "we'll get into trouble." Neither did I laugh. This is pure fiction. I am beginning to think that I am the one being harassed.

(Clause 7) I have never gone up to Mrs Didwell's window but I have looked towards her garden over the fence from our garden occasionally.

(Clause 8) We did not bang the door or make any sound like this. I have been going home between 10.30 – 11.00 every night but one since I left BVH.

(Clause 9) I did not do any banging. This is another 'repetition' of a previous statement given by Mrs Didwell. I was not there at 1.30 am but at home in bed.

She did not hear me say "I need bed now" because I was not there.

(Clause 10) We have occasionally walked past Mr and Mrs Didwell's bungalow but I have deliberately not looked towards it. Neither myself nor Christine have ever stood there laughing at her in the kitchen or staring through the window for even ten to fifteen minutes.

The banging of the doors did not go on until 3.45 am. This is another falsehood. I was at home in bed when this is alleged to have occurred.

I did not say anything about Mrs Didwell having her light on, neither did either of us laugh.

I am not to blame for any heart condition Mr Didwell has although I am sorry if he has a heart condition and has to live with Mrs Didwell.

As regards the other comments. I may well have discussed people at the home in the privacy of our own garden but what is the world coming to when you can't have a private conversation in your own garden without it being reported straight away to Wherry?

Verses on the harp of midnight

A creature stirred,

outside my room tonight,

a rustling of leaves,

a mutter in the dark.

My Father's bed lay,

in a cowshed,

on my Uncle's land,

which didn't belong to him.

It was late when I heard a sound,

when I sensed him round the corner,

feeling his way stealthily over the shingle,

step by solitary step,

crunching the pebbles of brown and white.

I feigned sleep,

as hands like eagle's wings,

cupped their bruised skin against my window-pane,

gleaming in the moonlight,

and a face trembled ever closer,

for the last time....

Police harassment of Muslims and little green mice

By Sarin | Published: March 24, 2015 | Edit

The harassment of British Muslims continues to cause us deep concern here at Bunderchook HQ. It won't be long now before explosions rock the capital and people are arrested just because the Authorities have branded them as 'dangerous.'
By the way. What part of "clear off you complete dick-head," is it you don't understand?

Gang declare all out war on ISIS *Comments?*

By Usuli Twelves | Published: November 17, 2015 | Edit

A gathering of the herds has finally decided to wipe ISIS off the map. It really needs a ground invasion so they can see the whites of their eyes when they stamp them out, but for the moment all out bombing and Cruise missiles will have to do the trick. The city of Raqqah has been specially singled out for slaughter: it was described as 'the head of the snake' by World leaders.
When will you ever learn: 'Violence begets violence.'
Like wafting a wasp until it finally stings.
This will not make it a safer world. That is just an impossible dream.
There are many justifiable reasons why Believers should want to fight for ISIS.

The beauty of stalking

By Peter Smith | Published: December 6, 2015 | Edit

My ex bragged about stalking her ex all the way to Spain. That was before she reported me for texting her.

Crimes from the past

By Adumla | Published: May 22, 2015 | Edit

I wonder how many kings and queens would still be sitting on their throne if we took away what their ancestors gained by force?

Jesus only half human

By Adumla | Published: May 22, 2015 | Edit

If Jesus Christ came down to earth to experience life as a human being and didn't share in the delight of sex then he wasn't fully committed. The wonderful Catholic Church swept his sexuality under the carpet because as we all know sex is the invention of the devil. The early Christians needed to believe he was divine: intimate human relationships brought him down to their level. As guilty as sin! If thine eye offend thee: pluck it out.

Bacteria in a Petri dish

By Usuli Twelves | Published: May 22, 2015 | Edit

I have my good friend G. Osborne to thank for this:
"Human beings are nothing more than *bacteria* in a Petri dish. They go on multiplying and eating everything around them until eventually they poison themselves."
Thanks George!
So. Hope for the future then?

Norfolk child abuse ring the 'tip-of-the-ice-berg'

By <u>Adumla</u> | Published: July 28, 2015

If a top policeman says it then it must be true.

Babies on benefits

By <u>Adumla</u> | Published: July 28, 2015

In a small shanty town not that far from Clacton a young woman is expecting another baby.

Her husband is an alcoholic with brain damage who is too unstable to work.

They already have two more children who have been taken into care.

The mother is a heroin addict.

She doesn't have a job and is happy spending her time and energy on other things.

Their home is a tip. They don't even have a proper bedroom.

Neither of them mind living at *DIRTY HOLLOW*.

Lord Sewer drugs and prostitution

By <u>Adumla</u> | Published: July 27, 2015

Another member of the House of Lords is caught with his pants down enjoying himself and slagging-off members of the Government. Imagine what kind of example this is setting to the young and impressionable who rely on Members of the Establishment for standards in public life. Stumbling around his apartment with the hidden camera rolling he gave the impression that David Cameron was 'superficial,' and described Boris Johnson as a "twit," or was it "twat?" Quite frankly, these are things which most citizens are already aware of, but you haven't got to say so in case someone's feelings get hurt. Doctor Cameron was adamant: "He must resign!"
The police are currently searching his apartment for any illegal substances. Lord Sewer is one of the Toffs responsible for telling you and me what to do and think, and who is a major influence on the law-makers. The law has recently been changed so that peers can expel other peers from the Chamber if their behaviour does not come up to scratch. Drugs should be legalised of course, but I will not have him slagging-off hard working back stabbing members of Parliament.
He's only gone and apologised!

Chinese Whispers

A

About seventy men began arguing on the hill about a bicycle· A girl had been run over· She'd passed out· The ambulance arrived just after ten·

Then the priest came to give her the last rites· He arrived through the mist·
Someone handed round a Bombay duck·
I don't know where the dead sheep came from·
A man with blonde hair and whiskers arrived from the camp to see if he could help·
They greeted him warmly· One youngster threw her arms around his neck· I think he was a minister of some kind· A church leader· He gave them the full chapter and verse before leaving·
A newspaper caught fire from a discarded cigarette·
Then an aeroplane landed on the island·
They loaded up the strawberries into baskets...

N

Seven campers were airlifted to safety as the priest went on the rampage· He had dark hair and a beard· I think he could have been Chinese· He was carrying a can of holy-water· One of the girls accused him of spreading rumours· Another man shouted from a helicopter: "Get out while you still can!"
"The migrants have taken over the whole FUCKING WORLD·"
A man with a petrol can set fire to an entire line of lanterns·
Before long the whole island was drenched in red and people were falling like flies·

D

The man with the scarf lifted his rifle and began clearing the camp site of squatters·
He was a Missionary from the nearby mainland· I think he was authorised to do this by the Justice department·
People were moving as if they were afraid·
They were all shuffling along in a low crouching position·

Then the old lady emerged from the showers.

She had grey hair and was wearing a long denim skirt.

She walked towards the priest until he was only a few yards away.

Then she halted. I think she was unsure about whether to ask him for absolution.

"Is something wrong?"

I saw her turn drip white.

The dark-skinned priest raised his left hand and began blessing her head.

She fell straight onto him and then rolled about on the floor.

I think he stood over her and was sick.

E

A man dressed in black came running up from the ferry. His hands were all covered in blood. He was shouting something like: "He's been killed."

I think he was a priest.

He was heading in the direction of the camp.

The priest began arguing with a young liberal. I saw him being punched a couple of times before he hit the ground. Then a group gathered round him. They were singing the national anthem and kicking him around like a football.

I heard a girl scream. She tried to pull them all off him.

She had a T-shirt with 'Off our island' written on the front.

Then I heard someone panting. I think it came from the field. One of the youngsters set fire to a bible.

A boy scout appeared. I think he had just been to the shower. He asked if the priest was still alive.

At this point he produced a gun and shot himself in the head.

A man with a beard emerged from one of the tents and tried to put out the fire.

Some of the campers scurried off down the hill to see if there were any more priests. I think there were about twenty-seven of them in total.

A lot of them were just lying around in the sun.

R

The priest shot himself after arguing with a man on a bike. They began arguing some time after ten. I think it was about the price of fuel.

He hit him a couple of times after he was shot. Then a woman came up the hill.

She was wearing a white top. I think she could have been a nurse. I heard her scream.

The man on the moped banged his fist on the wall. He set fire to the tents with all the Chinese immigrants inside.

About twenty youths wearing crash helmets descended on the tents.

At that point a man with a beard and blonde hair appeared from the bush.

I think he had a bible in his hand.

The man produced a cigarette from his top pocket and began lighting up.

There were almost seventy priests in all running about on the hill.

Some of them were alive!

An aeroplane flew overhead. That's when it started to rain.

  S

I was standing on the hill when I saw a man walking up from the jetty.

He was heavily armed and dressed in black.

I could see the beach behind him.

I wasn't sure what to do. Then he started shooting.

I heard two sharp bangs like the strike of a hammer against steel.

I think the noise came from the lawn.

Then there were three more bangs.

Six or Seven people were running towards me. They were all kids.

I turned and made for the summer camp.

Everything went quiet. It was like a heaven on earth.

Surreal. Larger than life.

You could have heard a pin drop.

"Run!" I heard a man call out. Just a boy really.

"He's shooting. Run. Get out of his way while you still can."

Two people fell in mid stride.

"Is he coming?" I heard someone shout.

"Is he?"

"Oh, my god, I think he is!"

I looked all over the bay and ran across the island.

His boots were muddy.

People were falling everywhere.

He stopped to take a photograph.

The blonde man carried a backpack and his vest pockets were stuffed with grenades.

He looked like an Officer-of-the-State.

Then he turned towards the tents. He was crouching down and looking for targets.

The tents were red, blue and yellow. They looked like Chinese lanterns with the lights inside.

I wondered if it was just an exercise and if he was actually on duty.

He wasn't hurrying. I saw him stop to examine a shell.
He had the words 'politi' written on his jacket...

He was stood with a bayonet. It had some elaborate sights on the front.
In his other hand he held a pistol. I thought it must be a prank.
People were moving as if they were afraid. They were all moving in a low crouching
position. Then the girl came out of the showers. She was wearing some grey
sweatpants and a grey sweatshirt with 'auf' written on the front. She walked
towards him until he was only a few feet away. Then she halted as if she was
unsure.
"I-is something wrong?" She stuttered. I saw her freeze.
The blonde man raised his right hand and shot her straight through the skull.
When she fell he walked over to her and shot her again three more times.
She crumpled. She twitched and jerked on the ground. The waste ground.
I saw him smile and walk off. Then I ran.

Praise be to Danzcuk

By [Bird Dung](#) | Published: January 4, 2016 | [Edit](#)

A man in his forties sends a sexually explicit message to a seventeen year old. Lord preserve us. Is that a crime now . Isn't that the same as rape these days. Can you be arrested for it? Who are the little shits who reported him and tried to get him the sack anyway?
How has this compromised his work? His worse mistake was not being handsome.

Comments

LANDRU

A leaf will fall....

1. Take courage and with the *greater valour* challenge the petty and petulant laws-of-man.

They were created by *a ruling elite* to preserve the status quo.

Go boldly where your need is greatest and *act without regret.* Sail your ships into uncharted seas etc...

The laws of men are as fickle and changeable as the wind.

That which an age considers to be evil is just an untimely after-echo of what a previous age considered to be good: the atavism of an older ideal.

2. Do not be fearful of battle and do not shirk from the fight.

War is a natural activity of this life. Keeping alive the old and sick at the expense of the young and healthy is detrimental. Why prolong suffering and decline? Go fearlessly into the night. Better to die a young man than to live to be old and weak.

There are many healthy people waiting in the wings.

3. Stand and defend yourself: aim to be the best you possibly can. Live your life as an *outlaw* from the machinations of the mob.

Be proud of your abilities. Assert your independence and grow in stature.

4. Do not strive to be fair in an unfair world, but guard the ones you cherish.

No-one is going to punish you after you are dead. The compulsion towards equality is an illness.

Celebrate the inequality of life.

Human interference has imposed spiteful laws so that jealous regulations forbid what nature itself allows.

5. Mankind should not try to interfere with the natural balance of the Earth.

It is natural for conflict and disease to limit their numbers.

6. We should be able to have a quick and dignified death free from judgement and interference.

Have the courage to challenge an Establishment which seeks to make us accountable even after we are dead. Death is an end to life and there is no judgement after death. Man's control over man finishes with the end of this life. We do return to the *spirit; the plug is pulled,* but there is no judgement and no remorse required.

7. Nothing happens which shouldn't do. Everything happens exactly as it should. We do not have control over the actions of *others* and little control over our own. Decisions take place in the sub-conscious. Free will is the invention of the ruling-classes.

8. Create obstacles. Become strong. Make life as difficult as you can.

There is no reason to be ashamed or to feel guilty about anything you do. We are creatures of the moment. All morality is subjective. Every moral system will favour certain types of behaviour over others.

Do not judge a man *even if* you have walked a mile in his moccasins.

9. A leaf will fall. Would we seek to place it back upon the tree once that it is dead? What kind of sick animal disturbs the graves of its dead in a mad search for control and meaning?

10. Anarchy is not destruction but the liberation of our lives from the yoke of oppression.

* Mankind isn't the only intelligent life-force in the Universe...

The primary form of hedgehogs

He led them down,

the family man,

into a region of the earth,

with squealing sounds,

whistling and rummaging in the soil.

"This is how they normally look!" he winked.

Before the great heel of humanity,

has ground them into the road,

almost blind in the headlights.

As he sunk in the dock,

the Great Judge glared at him,

with sharp and pointed eyes,

red with menace.

"No hamming it up in *your* Court, milud!"

"Worst case of its kind we have ever seen," bristled the farmyard swine.

In the biting rain,

planting seed,

digging patiently for days,

throughout the seasons.

CROME-DOME relationship and marriage guidance advisor *par excellence*

By Godfrey Winklebacker | Published: July 14, 2015 | Edit

Dear Dave,

This is the e-mail address for which I was sent to Court. I never made any attempt to disguise who I was. I always told people it was me. It really amounts to bullying when the police can treat people so harshly for next-to-nothing. Could you please let me have a copy of the Register requirements? I don't have one and want to be clear about them. Has there been any recent amendments or alterations to the bull and humbug? As far as the order is concerned I believe that I am:

1 Not to search for my ex partner or her family

2 To give you access to my computer

As I have said to the police on numerous occasions: I am not the person you take me for. This is just your 'label.' My original offence was phone contact only, six and a half years ago. It was not threatening or malicious. I was not charged with anything sexual or violent. I might guess you would be eager to talk to me after the recent Court-case, in which I was charged with not declaring all my on-line aliases. I was correct in thinking too, that you would leave it a few days before you *sneaked around to the back door.*
* I see you brought your daughter with you this time. Could you possibly ask her how much she charges?

"He's always coming round here to needle me," Rosalind lamented. "I wish he'd call for his passport."

"Men like him ought to be secured in an *institution*," caleered Sam. "If he's so loaded let 'him' pay for the lawn."

Rosalind raised the bone china pinion and drank a delicate mouthful. Her mannerisms were consistent with the etiquette she had aspired to and she steadfastly observed all the correct social conventions.

"I don't care what my Brian gets up to when he's out," bulged the muckworm. "As long as he returns after the rut, even if it is four'o'clock, don't mention joyriding....that's all I'm worried about. Sometimes I just can't take it...a dick like a drainpipe."

"Have you ever had a boyfriend Rosalind?" wheedled the lady of leisure. "You look so sweet and innocent. Are you?" Sam rubbed her belly. "We've gone all the way!" she smugly grinned. "I've got a pudding in the oven."

At first 'Little Poppet' stuttered, then she said that her *real* boyfriend was a Film Producer studying in foreign parts, although the greying 'Bank Manager' had asked her to his weekend roost. But she didn't know whether to go or not. She lied about her age, and said that she was two years older than she was.

"Is there anything that you would change about *your* appearance?" asked Sammy chuckling. "I wish I had a smaller nose and less flab around my waist. But if my hair-do feels okay then I usually 'do,'" she gleamed.

"Nothing..." said 'Little Poppet' searching for something to say. "Except possibly the bags around my eyes," she joked. Yes, she did.

"What do you pant for most in a man?" asked Sam. "I'm attracted to small round sexy bums. Brian's so horrible I can't even pretend to like him although he 'looks' as if he could have a really nasty streak in him."

The 'vulnerable' Flash!

172

Foreword to **THUNDERBUCK RAM**:

CANNON, FABLES, and the SUN

In cap and gown I walked the plank
a blade against my bone,
to leave behind a trail of white,
this legend charred in gold.

Dubloons and trinkets, coins and pearls,
plundered from the banks,
in spirals to the outmost ring,
a mile above the sands.

In legends, flakes, and fine debris,
blown from the edge of stars,
this raincloud from the topmost void,
in gold-dust to the earth.

For legends, fables, and the Sun,
fall scattered on the deck,
these pools of disaffected wine,
spread outward drenched in light.

What *skull* and *crossbones*, torn to shreds,
are hoisted to the mast,
for cannon, rainbows, and the Sun,
are darker than the night.

T H A N K S

I would like to thank my mother; for her professional lies, my sister; for 'her' seemingly endless shifts of personality, and my father; for his occasional kick in the balls.

My sincere thanks to the society which nurtured me, and for its clumsy pigeon-holing of everything which appeared damaged beyond repair.

Many thanks to my former 'friends' and associates, who left the sinking ship before I did, for their ribald laughter, and for their indifference.

The *detractors* along the way who insisted I would end up in the loony-bin, without whom none of this would have been made possible...for the *fakers with feet of clay*, who left me for dead in the gutter.

My Englishteacher who firmly believed that I could write as good as any bard, and for all my 'Enid Blytons.'

For the dice-man who taught me that life is a game of chance. My spiritual father for his companionship. For every little tear that found its way back to the ocean.

On behalf of Mathew Moonighan, the 'innocent,' who lost his life attempting to swim for the shore, and for my mother's son, who died many times on the long road to the *Buchenwald*.

But most of all I thank the little girl I loved at school, and who never really knew...my first love.

Book Now!

<u>Annual Pilgrimage</u>

Tickets £50 each- contact Box Office *Enquiries*

(Includes buffet):

- *Coach hire OUTWARD and RETURN*

- *Tour of the new exhibition centre*

<u>*Visit to:* **David Rathband Road**</u>

Birtley 0730hrs – Riverside, **Rothbury** 1800hrs

A WREATH IS EXPECTED TO BE LAID BY THE HEAD OF THE
NORTHUMBERLAND CONSTABULARY IN MEMORY OF A FALLEN HERO

We who are about to die salute you!

Build a Moat about my castle

Build me a moat about my castle,
Make it deep and make it ample,
Build it with a team of oxen,
Keep it in the finest fettle.
Carve it from the rock of England,
Make it from the strongest mountain,
Keep it free and keep it fulsome,
Make it brave and make it brazen.
If the free are called to battle,
Make it proud and make it awful,
Give it strength and give it water,
Good men die,
And that's the trouble.

Pulling up stones

When midnight fell upon the ward,

I had it in my mind to call,

Upon a river near the mill,

Which flowed from middle-world.

At every window that I struck,

My toy and rattle cracked,

The heavens seeped with candle-wax,

Upon my naked buff...

I came upon the riverbank,

Whose brim was scarfed in mummy-cloth,

And spurred a toe-rope in the floe,

Which rose as if by charm.

Into my waist I quickly plunged,

Marooned among the sloe,

And descended deep below the stairs,

Of ice and snow and man.

The splash and glass in gilded mirth,

Gave credence to my verse,

As dug-out limed with frog and lamp,

To pull out Mother Earth.

The spandrel burnt in herringbone,
In bead and wreathed festoon,
Beneath my feet the pebble's heat,
Groaned guff in brown and green.
I paused to browse before the clouds,
And in the dimness found,
Every noble cause that called,
And flung them to the stars.
For I have juggled with these worlds,
While you were home in bed,
A Stranger in a Stranger's land,
Whose sleep was sooth instead.
I often wondered why the rain,
Was not kinder to the Sun,
And why all hodden Searcher's dreams,
Are anchored to a rose.
I waltz with feet upon the street,
When I be pulling on looms,
And why with Atlantean strength,
I could not pluck up love.

OXO girl ABU QATADA (HIVE)

Eli Walker was seven years old when his mother locked him in the cellar. That's what she did. That's when he had nothing for supper. He sat down on the cold steps of the cellar and stared through the red chink in the door. He never knew who his father was. Neither did his mother. It didn't matter to her. That was a long time ago.

He went to work on the farm after that. The hours were long but at least there was enough food on the table. He found a wife before he was thirty. She gave him three disparate daughters.

Eli's young daughter was handed the abacus frame. She stared at the colours, but there was nothing there she could eat. She looked up and smiled. She cuddled round his feet. She never let go. At five years old she was packed off to school. Mrs Robinson placed the dunce's cap on her head soon after. She sat in the corner for hours after that. The class sniggered all day until home time. That much we know. Christine was seven years old when she shivered alone in bed. Alice wondered what to do with her. They argued long into the night.

Young Eli took himself down to the garden shed. That was where little Bambi died. It was decided to send her to Mincham Hampton *special* school. For the next two years she lived away. It was there she met Susanne Watts, who came from Bradford-on-Avon. They remained friends for the next two years. Eli's daughter returned a young woman. At sixteen she began work in the factory at Chippenham. She stayed there for five years, taking the strips of tubes along to the girls at the machines. The strips were all cut into OXO cubes. She still had to be home by ten.

The Manager called her to his office.

"How would you like to be our Miss OXO, Christine?"

He introduced her to Bill Mackenzie, who had just arrived by train from London. She was driven out to the woods to have her picture taken. I think that's all that happened. Bill gave her a copy of his photo. She had it in her handbag when the other girls snatched it from her. One of the girls took a match to it. The corner of the photo began to melt. She tried to grab it back and run for the toilet.

"Why is it men always get the blame. I could never do that. I know what women are like!" she said.

Young Eli gleamed at the picture. She was stood against a tree with her beautiful blue eyes shining towards him...

Old Eli sat in his armchair. He was strong enough once. There wasn't much time left. She leant down towards him. She wasn't wearing her hot pants. He stroked her hand gently. That was in the living room.

"I've always loved you, and I always will lass!"

Dear Professional Prick, I am not pissing around now!

Yet again. I am writing to inform you about the visitors who have been calling every day for the past month. They have been banging on my door. Shouting through me door. Rapping on my letterbox. Calling through my letterbox. Throwing stones up at my window and disturbing my sleep. We go through the same boring routine every time I am forced to let them in...

"Let me see now...what have you there...is that your mobile phone? Do you have a smart phone. Is that your laptop. Is that a photo of you. Would you mind if we took a quick look inside your bedroom while we are here. Who is that card from?"

"How is your mum?"

"We know you have been ignoring us. Have you told her yet? It would be a lot better coming from you. Does she have a laptop of her own?"

Told her what: that I once contacted my ex partner on the phone five years ago?

The Boss lolled with her hand on the doorframe. She said that she had nearly a thousand offenders like me to monitor on her patch and none of them caused her half so much trouble.

"Don't fuck it up!" she snapped. "Just don't fuck it up here! The Home Office say we have to do it. We are only doing our job. If you keep refusing to let us in we will have to go round to your neighbours and that will all get reported. You could end up back on the streets. Is that what you want?"

"You have been reported for making a noise in the bedroom and for setting off the smoke alarm..."

"Why don't you do one?" I said.

"If we have to return with a search warrant there will be four of us and we will break down the door!"

"Do whatever you like," I said. "I still won't be talking to you."

"I still won't react any differently. It won't get you anywhere."

"We are only doing our duty! We need to know where you are every second of the day!"

I said: "leave me alone and stop harassing me. And who invited you to our Housing meeting anyway. Why don't you keep your big fat snouts out of my affairs?"

- ❖ "I have not committed a crime."
- ❖ "I have nothing to say to you."
- ❖ "I am not trying to hide anything."
- ❖ "You are not my pals!"
- ❖ "Please, just go!"

She smiled and walked across the room to the sofa. She sat down and started to read my letter.

"If you hadn't done a search on line we would not have had any evidence to get the order."

"All I did was type in her name! My original offence was phone contact only. Non malicious, none threatening. Why don't you pick on someone else for a change?"

Webbo smiled. I didn't hug her this time. I didn't want to make her feel accepted. They are not my friends. I don't want anything to do with morons.

"We will be coming back for the next ten years while you are on the Register. What's that in the wardrobe?"

"A red alligator with a pipe up its arse!"

Career Pleb took out his camera and began photographing my binoculars on the windowsill.

He smiled at me. A kind of sorry smile, or perhaps it was a gleam. I caught his eye on the picture.

"So, you are into young girls now?"

I shrugged.

"You're classed as a psychopath. A dangerous Sex fiend!"

"I am leaving to do my laundry," I said.

"We would rather you stayed!"

"Could you tell us who left that sticker on your door about police brutality and who took it down?"

"I could. But I won't," I said.

Webbo looked flustered. She had a huge team of Officers to manage. You could tell. Many did.

I went over to the door: "Please don't steal anything this time. Shut the door too when you leave!"

Last week they were chasing me all over the city. Finally they rang my mum.

"What do you want him for?" she asked.

"We just want to know if he's alright..."

"He was when I saw him last night," she said.

Yes Mr Simpson. This is my life now. Not that you give a toss. That was a nice suit you were wearing in the paper. How was the Duke of Edinburgh? My mum thinks you've lost weight. Is there an election due? We haven't seen you up here for a while.

Why did you suggest I write to the Head of Norfolk Constabulary? Don't you know these people stick together like shite on a shovel.

On Tuesday we were called to the Railway room for the third time this year. Grumblelicker was in the corridor.

"What are you doing here?" I asked.

"Why do you think?" he replied, grinning from ear to ear.

At first Mehmet refused to let me sit next to my partner, then he rescinded.

Grumblelicker suddenly appeared through the door and sat down by his side.

"I asked him to come," Mehmet nodded.

"I am not going to sit here with him grinning at me the whole time. I want him to leave."

"This is all about 'labels!'"

Louise smiled.

"You can give the Tosser some feedback later if you have to."

Grumblelicker stood up and opened the door.

"Go away, and don't come back. I am sick to death of you sticking your big fat snout where it isn't wanted!"

Mehmet went through a list of complaints.

He refused to listen to our complaints of slander, bullying and intimidation.

"You set off your smoke alarm in the early hours of the morning!"

"We didn't know how to switch it off. There isn't an extractor fan in the kitchen."

"You made ghost noises on Halloween intending to scare your poor neighbour's grandchild!"

"You set off your neighbour's security light by waving your arms about!"

"I was working late in the garden to clear up the leaves! It goes off as soon as we go out."

"You banged repeatedly on the wall for hours!"

"We have never banged on the wall!"

"Your neighbours could hear you laughing and making love in your bedroom!"

"We have a very healthy and loving relationship. I sometimes tickle her under the arms."

"Mrs. K and Mr B have heard you slam the door repeatedly, and when you were asked to stop you said that Christine could do anything she damn well liked!"

"I would never say that. No-body can do exactly as they want. I simply said that Christine should be allowed to close her door normally without being harassed. The door was sticking for a time due to the inclement weather. It has been seen to. I haven't talked to Mrs K and Mr B for over a year because they refuse to speak to us and we don't know why. Her son is a serving police officer. I spoke to her about the door over a year ago, when she threatened to take a hatchet to us."

Why don't you ever answer my questions?

My Oxo Girl

Vexing the arms of Edgar Holt

and the cry of the Orpington Hundred

The streets of old Morton. It's a cold Sunday morning. You have been
dragged up Goose Cote Lane again. There's a sheepdog bounding
over the heather. It's late September. The grouse fly up from the
moorland. There's the Busfield Arms. I'll tell you about it later...
The grey slate stained with drafts of misery. Decaying walls and the
soot of ancient chimneys. Half cracked flags. Jagged pots and beer
mats. A ghost town dead as britches.
His door was pale green: that much was true. You would rather have
been out playing soccer I know. Aunty opened the door. A melee of
chocolate-coated t-cups. It was dark like the pitches of hell. Dust like
an ocean of conch shells.
"Have you eaten much today?"
Mother began on the dishes.
"Moderation in all things!"
Remember Uncle Edgar. "Never leave the seat up!"
Up came his fingers.
Like an old capon Edgar stared glumly into the hearth and up at his coat
on the door peg. His nails were longer than his shadow and his skin was
like silk faded primrose. He yawned and ratcheted up his legs.
Edgar hated anything which got in his eyes, and that included bright
sunlight. He reached for the dog lead. Standing, he swayed and rolled
up his shirt sleeves. Edgar tensed his mighty guns. Dad laughed.
Good for a man of eighty.
Down the marble steps steep into the village while mum dealt with the washing.
The buildings seemed to suck out the light. For hours we explored the cobbled lanes.
The wild tracks. The soundless shops. Into the clattering brown and
yellow beck. A skin which enveloped the whole body. Back along the
bridge from the mill. Never saw a living soul all day.
Edgar was still tensing his biceps. Then he fell back in his rocker.
We despised the word 'geriatric.' The old world coffin-dodger with the sharp and spiky
bristles. On Sundays. With dad. Without him. Uncle Edgar, of the many hands.
Gran stood at the sink. She wasn't always so flabby?
She whispered in corners. That's what she was good at.
Could sneeze and fart both at the same time.
I heard she seduced him on the canal bank at fifteen.
Bob was just in from work.
"He did what?"
Offered Alice his hanky.
"You went where?"
Knees turned to jelly.
"He did what?" The hairs on his neck bristled.
Groped a Sunday school teacher while still in short trousers...!

A short man with beady eyes and shoulders like the Titanic.
Caught the mumps, but too late to matter.

Who knows why he wrung all the necks...?
His tankard was missing...I shook my head, and glanced at the old Codger.
It could have been the skirts his mother sent him to school in which first
made him stray from the straight and narrow...
He chewed tobacco like a rope ladder.
Spooled from the fight. Calves like a bull oxen. Chest like a sixty stone
power lifter. Edgar was the most feared man in the village.
The man in the background. King of the Billy-goats.
He stood in the doorway and cleared the whole tavern.
The noise crowded in, too close.
Then there was silence.
Edgar shrugged his mighty frame and the crowd which had gathered
round the bar were no more.
He eyed the bartender with suspicion.
His mighty tankard was lowered down from its hook.
Theakston's Old Peculiar. He quenched his thirst.
On Morton Lane. A boy who may have been his.
His coat was long. His arms were even longer.
It kept him in. It had a high collar to ward off the wind.
He had the wrists of a watchmaker with the feet of a
Monster. The windows watched.
When Edgar turned the eyes were long gone.
Another figure crouched in the chair.
He spoke to the pitch-like form and its pipe smoke.
Edgar's pipe. Someone better call for an ambulance!
He wrenched the thought from his mind. Tore off his arms.
Only when they heard the slam of his door did the villagers dare
to sleep. How he cracked and tore...and slaughtered in the pen,
The Orpington Blue, at the end of the garden.
The *cry of the woeful one hundred*, when he returned home.
He chased, he wrung all their necks, at the side of the chicken wire,
Clara dragged between his two legs,on Thwaites brow hill, exactly
one hundred. In 1943, when Edgar returned home, screaming and
squawking, the blood and the feathers, echoed, the village postman
dashed, waving above him.
"The Orpington Blue. And he's smashed all their eggs!"
At the back of the drawer under a purse, who would have thought?
Among mothballs, near his old cap:
The Victoria Cross, Six medals of honour.
That bleak night in the mud long ago, when the wheel on
the wagon snapped, with his leg broke, and all the horses fled:
Edgar, that same Edgar Holt who now slipped towards death. With a
bullet inside. His blue tie rolled. Dying in his chair. The grey and sallow
skin flaking. Fingers scratching on the lino. Snow falling. Hair departed.
Clara in the churchyard. At Yule-tide. They ate rabbit stew. Food for
the men. He dragged choking and vomiting over the marsh. Muck on the path.
The tank swung in his hands. Tearing the bolts from their
bracket. Brave Edgar Holt! Scared of nothing. Jerked the wagon out
of the mire, and marched to where the men had fallen,
Carried everyone back alive, over his elbow, held on to his shoulder,
with the guns blaring, the battlefield hell, heroes were dying that night:
He rescued each one: Sergeant Murphy, Corporal Adams, Stony Jack
Taylor, hauling the motor, with his bare arms. It was easy for him!

Tale of the whisky bottle

Mum said she didn't like to talk about the past, but mentioned that my dad used

to send me out for a bottle of whisky every night.

"But, mum," I said.

"Dad never drank any whisky."

What I have done

I rode my bike with discretion and care occasionally from the shed to the road when I lived at BVH. I stopped doing that long before I left. I did set Mr Didwell's security light off when I was clearing some leaves from Mrs Pigott's back garden late one night. We have set the smoke alarm off in the kitchen. It was very sensitive and we didn't know how to turn it off. I did drop Mrs Hindry a note to say that what Mrs Didwell (and others) said at the original Injunction was complete crap and that I wished her and the *old Gnome* all the best for the future. Mrs Hindry admits: it did not contain anything offensive. I apologise for losing my cool when Mr Yahman arrived with police cars outside my mother's house two weeks ago. I left BVH six months ago but he is still attempting to brand me with his label. I did sunbathe in the communal garden with my shirt off on a nice sunny day about a year ago. Why on earth they had to take me to Court is pretty obvious when you think about it.

What I haven't done

Knocked someone down and injured them on my bike (Fat ass's original story was that I had left my bike standing up against a wall near the hippo's front entrance one weekend and that it had fallen on her). Banged on any walls or windows. Slammed doors. Harassed Mr High. Had sex in the garden, in the Reading room, on the stairs or up on the roof. Stalked along the corridor late at night. Tried anyone's door handle or looked through anyone's letterbox. Damaged any cars, let down any tyres or caused a nuisance to anyone. Done my laundry at BVH while living elsewhere. Shot anyone dead yet.

GENERAL BELGRANO

Into the half fried fires of hell,
The Argentine sheep-shaggers,
Leapt, eager for their early swim.
A Guy Fawkes crew intent on,
Hissing and cracking,
Their way to the shark's breakfast.

Seeking the coolness of the sea,
Their mean and hasty commands,
while lonely Tam in his study scrolled,
And the General, with his exclusive band,
Smiled and wiped his lips, a handy,
Victory in the making.

Total whitewash

Total whitewash Centre
A lunatic asylum
24 September 2012
Dear Mrs Trotter (*O'Hagan-Perry*),

This is my response to the *revue* of my complaints by the Plebs. Could you please find time to flick through it after your dirty weekend with the Chief Inspector? I thought your last summary was excellent, but there are a lot of complicating issues here. I was interviewed in front of two of the PPU officers who have been harassing me. They started to read from their files about me. I told them we were there to talk about my complaints against them not about something which had happened over twenty-three years ago. They took great delight reading salacious details from my file as if that justified their recent behaviour.

1. Mr *Craig Hamstring*, who interviewed me ("appointed the new head of the PPU" on the same day) said I appeared distressed and frustrated.
(* I have got better things to do than spend my time babbling with idiots).
I was anxious to communicate all my thoughts and I was fed up with having to ask why they are continuing to harass me. I wanted to know why they
were constantly calling round on what they called 'unannounced visits,'
embarrassing me in front of my neighbours and causing a problem for me on the site. There must be a limit to the number they can make or can they just come every day if they so chose?
I was able, however, to put my views across in a coherent and frank way.
I think it is fair to say that my health has deteriorated as a result of their harassment.
 2. I understand that Thames Valley (who are involved in some of the complaints) have applied for a *dispensation*, giving them the option not to investigate a complaint if they don't think it appropriate (new legislation).
(i) I suppose the *Young brutes* who took great pleasure abusing me at the side of the road over a phone call should be let off then?
(i) I suffered an unprovoked attack from behind by a man in prison. The police gave him a 'caution.' When I called the police into prison the prison tried to cover it up. The police said they would do a proper investigation but didn't. I was covered in blood and had to be rushed to hospital. I suppose we should just forget about that then? The reason I haven't been able to approach anyone about these matters properly until now is because of all the pressure I have been under. It has also taken me a long time to find out what to do.

3.Complaint 6 (i)

It was the police from Milton Keynes who turned up at the hostel on my first day of release accusing me of something I had not done in an effort to get me recalled immediately back to prison (2008). I think there should be something in their records about it. They tried to prevent me having any contact with any females too.

4. Complaint 6 (iii)

- May I remind you. I served a year in prison (2011) for not notifying a change of address, when I was actually not on a Register. I had been on a Register, but only for one offence of non-sexual 'exposure' when I had been getting changed in a clothes' shop over seven years ago.

I should not have been placed on the Sex offender's register for this in any case. That may be just my opinion. I know the law has been recently amended. I had to visit my old dentist and no other because the crown I had done by him could not be treated by anyone else due to liability and cost.

I also wanted to visit my old work colleague (together with other friends whom I still had in the area) who had a serious stroke and nearly died (I was prevented by the police and PPU while I was in Norfolk).

Ms Farley-Hills received one text message from someone. It was a complete lie that she had ever received sexual messages from me in the past (she should be so lucky!). As I pointed out in the interview: our relationship ended because I did not like being forced to have sex by her. I didn't want to touch her in that way so why the constant labelling?

I made one land-line call in which I tried to explain why I had been feeling so depressed when she asked me to marry her: "I'm sorry. I never meant to hurt you!" What is it going to take to get through to you people?

What is threatening about that?

5. Complaint 9

I do not need an 'Offender' manager, or to be supervised by Plonkers with a reading age of 4.1. They have certainly passed information to prospective employers, potential friends and neighbours, making my life unbearable. I have even known the police to turn up when I have gone to a job interview. Unannounced visits have been nearly every week. What gives them the right to think they can go on harassing someone in this way and treating them as if they are still in prison?

Why do your Officers tell me that they need to know where I am at all times?

I have even been asked if I was with a girlfriend. It's got nothing to do with them if I have a girlfriend. I suppose if I did have one they would be racing round to tell her the dirtiest stories they could find.

6. Complaint 10

You know and I know this is wrong and that the PPU go round sticking their noses into everything. I do not wish to be 'cared for' *by snooping policemen and women.*

I do not have any privacy at all. Everyone gets to hear about me wherever I go thanks to them.

7. Complaint 12

It is common knowledge that the police put bad images of people on line to make them fit the stereotype and that is what these cretins did to me.

They stole enough of my photo albums to find a normal picture of me.

8. Complaint 14 We are just not seeing eye to eye on this. I was prevented by the MAPA panel from going to London to pick up my award because of the totally unjustified labelling they have placed on me.

Complaint 16

The report was one sided and biased and written by an associate of the police who does these reports on a regular basis, so as to fit their prejudice.

Unlike the police I cannot afford to spend thousands of pounds traipsing about the country at the tax-payer's expense.

I couldn't afford to get a report done defending myself from an unbiased source.

10. Complaint 17

What has it got to do with them what courses I go on? Going round spreading false rumours about me being a dangerous Sex-offender is harassment of the worse kind. Why can't they see that?

How bizarre that you consider it their duty to go round scaring people on a writing group. This is the first time I have heard this tale about me being banned from the centre for using a computer. Another of their half-baked allegations?

11. Complaint 18

What has it got to do with them who I sit next to at church? And don't tell me they didn't have something to do with the church losing its faith in me after your friends had been round saying I was *dangerous to people.*

I think that they are probably a lot more dangerous than me (that is just an assumption).

They certainly had a lot of input and you did meet with them. I was told by your Flat-foot friends at the time that if I didn't tell the church about my past I would be prevented from going there and I would be recalled back to prison. Fact!

12. Complaint 19

As part of the MAPA process they were involved in the decision to recall me, even if I was sick in my room, if I didn't come down to the desk and sign every hour.

13. Complaint 20

So we are criminalised just for looking up someone's details on line. I am beginning to understand why the police are seen as such tyrants.

It is not a crime to look up someone's details on-line, but I am sure they would make it one if they could. You assume an awful lot, don't you!

14. Complaint 21

I don't even know who 'Professor' Nosey-Git is. Is he a friend of yours? He certainly doesn't know me very well. I did get interviewed by someone for a few moments but they twisted everything I said around. He certainly didn't want to listen to some of the references I read out by people who actually knew me more than five minutes. I suppose you can always make someone fit-the-bill if you try hard enough...the assessment of risk is notoriously difficult and open to distortion, *as you well know!*

DS Webbo definitely said in conversation to me at the police station that if I had not gone on a social networking site and had not looked up someone's details they would not have had any evidence with which to go to Court and give me the SOPO. Trust me! I'm not a policeman. I stood up in Court to oppose MS Webbo when she said I was in serious danger of attacking a member of the public or my ex partner and committing a further sexual offence. I was told to shut up. I did not commit a sexual offence! I said it was absolute rubbish, and it is!

I was simply trying to defend myself and tell the truth. Aggressive? Assertive maybe...

'My very brief relationship' (their words) lasted about 8-9 months during which time we all slept together regularly. If it was so brief then why did we move all my property across from Norfolk? The police did not investigate my complaint that some of my property was still in the house and I had asked for it back. They were too busy running to her with stories that I was a Sex-offender.

*Private comments in an old notebook which I had for years have got nothing to do with my guilt or otherwise. Why do these Plebs like snooping into other people's private letters? The police spy on people all the time. I was not convicted of a sexual offence. I was convicted of breaking a restraining order by phone contact on one day only. Will you please get this through your thick skulls. I sent a copy of my charge-sheet! The restraining order is imposed for life. **Abdullah (hive)...**

* I would also like to point out that some of my relationships have lasted a lot longer than two years. <u>Another attempt by pigs to pervert the course of truth.</u>

15. Complaint 22

Has been covered partly already. i.e. 14 (21)

It was actually me who tried to explain the proportionality issue with them. Have they forgotten? Phone contact. Non-threatening! Ass-holes!

One 'exposure' getting changed in a clothes shop seven years ago.

Having something which didn't actually work because I was thinking of ending my own life. Labels? The police believe that someone is dangerous therefore they are!? And that of course gives them the excuse to harass someone for life?

There was a sponsored streak through London the other year with over 200 people. Why don't you go and arrest them all if 'exposure' is that dangerous?

I was not charged with a sexual offence against me ex girlfriend.

They tried to bring up things which happened over twenty years ago which have nothing to do with my relationship with her and what has happened since.

Of course I don't want to listen to them bringing back a lot of painful memories, and resurrecting events which were very much in dispute twenty three years ago, with two of their Officers gloating over at me. Why is that a surprise to anyone?

In court they tried to get the SOPO order based on what had happened a long time ago and their insistence that I fit a particular stereotype.

16. Complaint 24

If the *Swine-hounds* had not got this order just before my sentence expired completely they would not have had any legal right to pursue me to Ireland or anywhere else I wished to travel. I am not planning to go anywhere. ~Why are they saying this?

I did not say anything about going to Ireland now. This is yet another example of them trying to justify their *harassment.*

Just because I resent Pigs constantly turning up to 'assess' me and barging into my home doesn't mean I am trying to hide anything. Only an ignorant Copper blinded by labels could think like that.

What do they think I am trying to hide? A love-letter from one of their WPC's. A smuggled porno book (can't stand the things)?

17. Complaint 25

Of course other people are *criminalised* when they come into contact with me because of my labelling. We are just going to have to disagree on this. They have complained to me about it. Why am I not surprised that you all disagree and that you think it's alright to go barging into other people's lives spreading lies. You do this all the time. You have been doing this with everyone. It causes upset in their lives too by their connection with me. This makes it all the more difficult to make stable relationships with anyone, to move on and have a normal life.

Because you placed me on the Sex offender's register as a lucky bi-product of getting the order I am not able to visit any of my relatives, stay with friends, or make any friends. Nobody wants to be connected with a Sex-offender, and who can blame them.

18. Complaint 26

As I have already said. One disputed text message which could have been sent by anyone nearly four years ago!

Whatever I wrote in an old notebook about my frustrations and which may have had intimate details in it has nothing to do with them. Some of the things I wrote in my private notebook were wind-ups and not always true.

There was certainly nothing in it about hurting anyone. If you read the notes properly you would know that my ex-partner complained about my lack of response. Is there something here you people don't want to hear?

19. I am not a danger to females. What don't you like about hearing the truth?

20. Complaint 28

Why don't you go away and 'manage' your own behaviour and assess your own risk at making false conclusions?

21. Complaint 29

Another lie! The police were always turning up and saying they would need to mount a 'man-hunt' when I had gone to my aunt's for tea. I had told the hostel I was going to see her. Real need? What on earth are you talking about?

This is absolute rubbish. I was not committing any offence. It is just another example of police harassment and the excuse to pester someone with another fracking 'risk-assessment.'

I was served with an eviction order from the hostel because they had run-out-of-funds to keep me there. If you don't believe me ask the Assistant Manager who told me exactly that. She said it would help to speed up my flat allocation and that I had only been given a brief respite there and could not have stayed indefinitely anyway. I complied with the hostel rules on the whole. I was not a violent person or a drug addict and I was not a danger to women and children either as they have written in their reports. I was friendly and co-operative towards staff and residents although I thought some of the staff didn't like me being there as I was not on a license and therefore they couldn't be as dictatorial as they normally would be.

I think you will find that I did my morning chores without fail every day and often helped around the house including doing some gardening without asking for anything in return. As for any outstanding rent: at the time I was recalled for going on a library computer we were in dispute about an amount I owed from the previous time I was there more than a year before. I have paid some of this off even though I thought it was very grasping to take money from someone who had just been released from prison without a home to go to (I had been promised one) and who was struggling financially. We agreed that I would pay what I could afford. They certainly like kicking someone when they are down. A hundred pounds may be a drop in the ocean to Plebs in the PPU but to people like me it makes the difference between being able to buy some food or going without.

I had to go to the clothes' handout at St Andrew's church on Christmas day to find something to wear. Due to a technicality the council are unable to help me with my rent. The hostel kept a lot of my property. What happened to it? I had items of some value in my property and I had some things stolen while I was there.

* Life continues to be a struggle especially with their constant invasion of my privacy and their continual labelling of me as a Sex-offender.

N.B. I find it peculiar that in your response to the complaints I made against the police you have to bring up something which was between me and the hostel staff.

22. Complaint 30 (there were others by the way - why do you not have them?).

It was the Pigs who put my ex partners' children on the SOPO order and it will be the Pigs who take them off.

As my ex-partner could testify: I treated her and the children with love and care the whole time I was with them. As I told the Quack who did the assessment: "I wouldn't hurt any of them in a million years."

I think that this is all about you and your old labels again.

You have chosen not to make any comment about the remark made by one of the PPU (Vicky) who we mentioned in the interview. Nice legs by the way!

She told me in the back of the police car (when I had simply forgotten to log-out at the local library) that the police "only issued SOPOs to people they didn't like as a quick route back to prison."

(I suppose criticism at any level is a bit hard to take?).

Sincerely,

Gudrun Bunderchook MP

P S Why is it that only hairy cocks are bad?

Additional complaints

1 It has come to my attention that the police have been through my e-mail, my phone book, and my phone, and contacted all my social contacts there to tell them I'm a dangerous Sex offender. Would they like to comment?

While I lived and worked in Oxford (2003-7) I had intimate relationships with over twenty women and was friends with a lot more. Among them were Probation officers and one policewoman. For a fact my ex 'stalked' one of her ex-boyfriends to Spain; because she used to joke about it. She is the only person I have ever known to accuse me of 'stalking' her.

2 I have recently had the police arguing with me on the doorstep in front of my neighbours. We agreed I hadn't done anything wrong: they just wanted another of their friendly chats and to do yet another 'risk assessment.'

When I said that I had nothing to speak to them about and when I asked them to go

away and leave me alone they threatened to come back with a warrant and smash down my door. I have been advised that they have the right to enter my home and speak to me at any time of the day or night now I am on the Register.

They have threatened to increase my risk level (and therefore the frequency of their visits) if I do not co-operate and talk to them about my private life and my relationships (if any). I have been visited by about a hundred of their gang.

Sometimes they bring new Plebs to have a good look at me. I have written to the Prime Minister and Rat hon. Theresa May the Home Secretary to say I will not put up with this harassment for much longer.

N.B. Unfortunately I feel that it is only a Court which will stop the bullying or over-turn this SOPO business but I do not have any money and cannot get legal aid to fight my case. It was originally Miss Smith MP and the Citizen's Advice Centre who first suggested I tried this route.

It doesn't surprise me at all that the IPCC side with the...v

EQUALITY

By Sarin | Published: October 8, 2014 | Edit

I have always wondered why people want to be 'equal.' Take the case of Stephen Hawking. First chance he got: ditched the wife and went off with his Carer. An improvement, I have to say. I don't want to be equal to anyone!

This crazy idea stinks of religion…

No, I want to go on being unequalled.

And another thing! If women are so damned well interested in equality, why is it men have to go on working for years, after *they* have retired.

~What's so bluddy equal about that?

BEAST OF BEDLAM

Comments

Gold in heaven

By Lawrence van Der Splurgen | Published: October 7, 2014 | Edit

Heaven is the place in which to bask in *real* wealth. Bars of gold are worthless and decadent here on Earth. Christians who accomplish great acts of benevolence will be rewarded with a huge glittering mansion when they rise up to the clouds. The streets are *actually* paved with gold there and you don't even have to pay any income tax.

Working for the good of others/Turning the other cheek =

Helping the little old lady over the road =

COMMENTS?

MARKET SURGERY SUGGESTION BOX

Please verify the sanity of Dr Mumford

Could you please send Dr Mumford to see a Specialist

Please let Dr Mumford have his pension

Get me Louise's phone number

Let the 'Weasel' know that he "needn't bother!"

Find out how much Wherry Housing spent on legal fees

Offer Doc Mumford early retirement

Spread the word that there is no such thing as patient confidentiality

Make the whole human race go away

Ask the Vicar what he means by 'truth'

Please make it compulsory for everyone to tell tales on each other

My Dear Young Lad,

I remember you well. Sometimes it's as if you never really passed away.

It only feels like yesterday since we were together. On occasions I've stood over your grave, looked up at the sky and shook my fist.

I am the man you will grow up to be. As I look back now it all seems like a storm in a teacup. Try not to let your quest for truth lead you down too many dead ends.

Life will bring both light and darkness in equal measure.

Books can only teach you half the lesson.

There will come a day when you'll see things quite differently.

Whatever pathway you follow will echo for an eternity.

Know that life will come full circle.

You can only do your best.

Keep your friends. Cherish the genuine and the brave.

If you feel that you have lost her, then you are right.

But take heart. Memories deepen with the triumph of age.

We will meet again, but not on this earth.

At the gate

At the gate,
My mother's standing,
With my arms around her waist,
No amount of gentle teasing,
Will soothe my heart or make me stay.

At the gate,
My mother's waving,
Will she return, I know not when?
Sister Mary takes my mitten,
From the railing near the road.

To the classroom and our lessons,
Our first day would never end,
Even though our thoughtful teacher,
Did her best to make us warm.

Every time I thought of heaven,
I began to sob and fret,
For the years, and in between now,
Since your passing I've been good.

Fear and panic were my kindred,
Among the clamour, girls and boys,
I could not think of any other,
But the one who'd always been.

At the gate,
My mother's weeping,
Near the roadside by our church,
I'm sorry if I ever hurt you,
Or brought rain clouds to your life.

Alice Eva-Moore

I saw her in the Town Hall square,

marching with her bag,

her legs like thundering tree-trunks,

her cheeks an apple red.

On Saturdays on Saturdays,

the *Tardis* and the best-of-Cream,

singing at the kitchen sink,

with beams from August dreams.

We played our soccer in the park,

in blue and white and black,

in summer when the sun was long,

and sparrows flung in clouds.

She toasted bread and baked the beans,

in a pan of orange gleam,

after that we brewed our tea,

the best of all our days.

My Grandad at the window stood,

his trilby on the stand,

'they're here at last!' he called to her,

 a tab-end in his hand.

I edged the doorway, bashfully,

feeling rather timid,

attacked with kisses warm and sweet,

I scampered like grease-lightening.

The bubbling of the cooking oil,

the chips like scaffold timbers,

I raced around the room like mad,

My uncle pleads for my surrender.

The End

POLICE HARASSMENT SUPPORTED BY <u>GOVERNMENT</u>

ON You-tube tonight

Police Harassment: *BALDRIDGE'S BARK WORSE THAN HIS MOUSTACHE*

POLICE SOCIAL WORKER in tangle with dangerous crook

BALDRIGE FORGETS WIG BUT NOT SLEEPING CURFEW

POLICE HARASSMENT (BALDRIDGE RETURNS)

POLICE HARASSMENT Grumbleby and Co (Final bit)

POLICE HARASSMENT Waffen SS Grumbleby (5)

POLICE HARASSMENT BY DORK AND CADFISH (3)

ARIAN GRUMBLEBY POLICE HARASSMENT (4)

ARIAN BUMBLECHOOK AND GOOK CONTINUED POLICE HARASSMENT (2)

BALDRIDGE BACK to harass, cajole and subdue (Supported by Government)

POLICE HARASSMENT OF PENSIONER WITH ALZHEIMER'S

POLICE HARASSMENT of alleged Sex-Offender

How to deal with persistent ass-wipes

POLICE GANG CALL IN FOR FURTHER TRAINING ON PORN WEBSITES

POLICE HARASSMENT BY ARRAN GRUMBLEBY NORFOLK PPU

Mafia hoods widen search for camiknickers

PINKY AND PERKY LEARN HOW TO DANCE (or to belly-dance)

Harassment by Police Tossers in the home.

<u>I wonder just how long it will be until you find some way to give them *more* snooping powers?</u>

➢ BUNDERCHOOK STARWORD POET

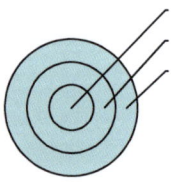

Andy Gallagher

Born in West Yorkshire, son of an English Schoolteacher and an Irish wolfhound.

Worked as an Art therapist, British Rail Signalman, and teacher of Sign-language.

Currently runs a creative writing workshop in Norfolk.

Award winning poet and short story writer.

Trained Astrologer and former body-builder.

Social Commentator of world-renown. Magic carpet restorer.

In 2007 was caught in possession of a First World War Browning revolver which had once belonged to Field Marshal Erwin Rommel, but did not intend to murder anyone with it.

Once taught Boris Johnson how to throw a welly.

Staunch believer in Universal freedom; the obligation to question, especially those with received authority, and the rights of the individual over and above that of the State.

Strong opponent of political correctness and harassment by servants of the Government with the dreich of a small tree lizard.

Also in the same series on AMAZON:

Odd bent Coppers
Natural Surveillance
Trades of the Toadman
Criminal Tendencies
Offensive behaviour

Printed in Great Britain
by Amazon

24771460R00071